Armed
for
Battle

A Balanced Approach to Spiritual Warfare

Armed for Battle

Peter N. Lundell

Beacon Hill Press of Kansas City
Kansas City, Missouri

ISBN 083-411-8807

Printed in the
United States of America

Cover Design: Paul Franitza

Library of Congress Cataloging-in-Publication Data

Lundell, Peter N., 1959-
   Armed for battle : a balanced approach to spiritual warfare / Peter N. Lundell.
     p. cm.
   Includes bibliographical references.
   ISBN 0-8341-1880-7 (pbk.)
   1. Spiritual warfare. 2. Christian life—Wesleyan authors. I. Title.
BV4509.5.L86 2000
235'.4—dc21

                                                       00-045421

10 9 8 7 6 5 4 3 2 1

To my wife,
whose prayer shakes the heavens.

Contents

Foreword

THE CHURCH OF JESUS CHRIST is at a remarkable place here at the beginning of the 21st century. The potential for accelerated evangelistic growth worldwide has never been greater in the history of the Church.

I know it is a calculated risk to use the adjective *accelerated* when we realize that the evangelistic harvest of the 1990s was unprecedented. I think of China and Indonesia and India and Brazil and Nigeria and Argentina and the Philippines and Ghana and Guatemala and many other places. While no one knows precisely, reasonable estimates of the number of individuals being born again have reached a figure of up to 140,000 per day. While the population of the world is increasing by 1.6 percent annually, the number of born-again Christians worldwide is increasing at over 6 percent per year.

However, this exciting news of the spread of the gospel does not describe all areas of the world equally. North America is one of the regions where Christianity is more or less holding its own, and it has been for several decades. Why is this the case? Why haven't we seen here what we have been seeing in Guatemala or Nigeria? I believe that the major answers to these questions are found in this remarkable book, *Armed for Battle: A Balanced Approach to Spiritual Warfare*.

Peter Lundell puts his finger on two spiritual principles that can release the extraordinary power of God onto our own nations: holiness and holy war.

For reasons the author explains in detail, we North Americans have fallen far behind our brothers and sisters in the third world in our understanding and application of holy war. The apostle Paul tells us that the reason unbelievers do not come to

Christ is that the god of this age has blinded their minds (see 2 Cor. 4:3-4). He goes on to tell us that our warfare is not against flesh and blood but against spiritual principalities and powers (see Eph. 6:12).

As you read *Armed for Battle,* you will clearly see that we Christians in North America need to move to a new level in aggressively pushing back the forces of Satan in order for God to do everything He wants to do on our continent. You will realize that the call to holy war is not just a fad, but it is a strategic biblical mandate that we need to take seriously.

Those in the Wesleyan tradition already know that personal holiness is a biblical mandate, and that is the second outstanding and essential emphasis of this book. My theological training was in the Reformed tradition, but when I began to move out into areas of spiritual warfare some years ago, I soon learned that the Reformed doctrine of progressive but incomplete sanctification was not adequate. I realized that if I was not meeting the biblical standard of personal holiness, I was opening wide gaps through which the attacks of Satan could hit their mark. It did not take me long to switch my position to Wesleyan Holiness, not only in theory but also in practice. My life and my ministry have never been the same since that change.

True personal holiness and aggressive holy war are a combination that the devil cannot possibly resist. That is why I believe *Armed for Battle* is an extremely important book, coming out at just the right time. Let's learn and apply these biblical principles and experience the power of God in North America that is already being poured out in other places. If we do, we can be a generation of destiny.

> —C. Peter Wagner
> Chancellor, Wagner Leadership Institute

Preface

MANY PEOPLE WHO CONFRONT the spiritual forces of evil, or what I will call "powers of darkness," desire clearer biblical direction and need deeper Christlikeness in their lifestyles. One of those people has been me. This battle demands that our very lives be set apart to the Lord. Thus, I call it "holy warfare." Scripture makes clear that this warfare is more about living a life of love for God and people than it is about power. Yet in living such a life, we see that it's also about fully exercising the power and authority God has vested in us.

The Wesleyan perspective has not been heard much in this arena, and I hope this book will give it a voice. In so doing, I hope the Scripture and the hand of God will be clearer and more powerful in your own spiritual battles. The victory is yours in Christ.

1

The Call to Holy Warfare

"WHAT'S GOING ON HERE?" I, the missionary, asked myself over and over. The unreasonable resistance to the gospel, opposition from non-Christians, inexplicable depression, backbiting and division in the church, and a sanctuary burned by an arsonist left me more than suspecting that my wife and I had run straight into the midst of some very dark spiritual powers. What were we to do?

HOLY WARFARE

Throughout history many nations and groups have claimed to be fighting "holy wars" of one sort or another. But few if any wars fought between political powers can genuinely be said to be holy. Invariably, it is simply self-interests of a nation or group that are at stake. Only one kind of war can truly be said to be holy: war that is explicitly fought for the kingdom of our holy God against demonic powers that oppose His kingdom and people. In the Old Testament, holy warfare was fought with swords of steel. Since New Testament times, holy warfare has been fought with the Sword of the Spirit—the Word of God.

In discussing a Wesleyan approach to confronting powers of darkness, one may well ask, Is this something Wesleyans ought to deal with in the first place? We may find an answer by looking to John Wesley himself. When speaking of "evil angels," he says, "Highly necessary it is that we should well understand what God has revealed concerning them, that they may gain no advantage over us by our ignorance; that we may know how to wrestle against them effectually."[1] According to Wesley, then, we should not only understand what Scripture reveals about powers of darkness but also know how to effectively "wrestle against them." Such was the apostle Paul's intent in Eph. 6. This book is an attempt to help us in that direction.

When we bring the gospel to those under the grip of the enemy, we often encounter inexplicable resistance or problems. Could the reasons and solutions have anything to do with the spiritual world? What about the driving forces behind social immorality, family breakdowns, crime, even personal temptations? Church fights and splits are all too common, and so are the reasons behind them. Could there be spiritual reasons that are not often enough recognized and dealt with? As a pastor, I meet with Christians who feel they or people they know are under some kind of spiritual attack—and often they are. This book will deal not so much with personal demonization of individuals as with the influence of demonic spirits in the deception of and opposition to the people and kingdom of God. The purpose of this book is not to theologically discuss the problem of evil but to recognize that as God allows sin and evil, He also supplies us with the means of victory.

When my wife, Kim, and I returned home from missionary service and came to our church in California, we found ourselves arguing and getting upset about things in a way that we normally would never have done. It went on for a couple of weeks, and we were both very troubled by it. We started a home cell group, and there we were told that every pastor in memory at this church (there had been quite a few) had had problems with marital conflict. Some were convinced that Satan had tried to destroy this church in many different ways, and all agreed that every pastoral couple had in some way been under some kind of attack, though no one was sure why or what could be done.

Kim and I had been through this sort of thing before. First we had the group pray for God's peace and protection over us. When we got home, we set our disagreements and feelings aside, joined hands, and agreed with each other in heartfelt prayer that we were one in Christ, that no evil powers would deceive us or get between us, that our home and marital relationship would be covered in God's protection, and that His peace and joy would reign. The fact that a large Mormon church stood directly across the street from our house made the prayer feel even more urgent. Since that time the problems have ceased, and joy has reigned in our home. But, as Eph. 6:18 teaches, we continue to be "alert" in prayer.

First Cor. 15:57 says that God "gives us the victory through our Lord Jesus Christ." And in 2 Cor. 2:11 Paul says that "we are not unaware of [Satan's] schemes." Many times we believers, as sanctified as we may be, could have gained victory or helped others gain victory but didn't—because we were unaware of Satan's schemes. Perhaps it was because we didn't take the devil seriously or perhaps because we simply didn't know. In *Exploring Christian Holiness,* Richard S. Taylor states, "We are involved in a holy warfare. It is a real war, not a chocolate-soldier make-believe. From this war there is no rest and no discharge until God himself transposes us from the field of battle to the throne of victory."[2] As long as we are in this world, we would do well to follow Wesley's advice that "we should well understand what God has revealed" concerning the powers of darkness.

THE HOLY SPIRIT AND POWER

Donald Hohensee questions those who claim the infilling of the Holy Spirit without a resultant holy living. But he goes on to say, "It is also reasonable to question those who profess to be purified when there is no empowering. In recent years I believe the Wesleyan Movement has put more emphasis on the purifying aspect and not sufficient on the empowering."[3] When looking at the power of the Holy Spirit manifested during the Holiness revivals of the past century, for example, we can see what Hohensee is talking about. The sweeping power of the Spirit convicted masses of people of sin and transformed their lives in an act of God that overcame the powers of darkness in people's lives. How much do we experience that power?

Jesus said, "You will receive power when the Holy Spirit comes on you; and you will be my witnesses" (Acts 1:8). How many of us have neglected the empowerment of the Holy Spirit? How many of us have been satisfied with personal holiness and not pursued the truth and power of God toward breaking the hold of the evil one over people around us? This same Spirit is "the Spirit of truth" (John 14:17), for the Holy Spirit's power is founded on God's truth. And the power is for the purpose of effective witness. The truth is that God is almighty, Jesus conquered sin, death, and the devil's work, and we are children of God, who exercise His authority in Jesus' name. Effective witness demands an awareness of the devil's schemes and the exercise of the Holy Spirit's power in overcoming them to the glory of God.

OUR WARFARE IS DISTINCTLY HOLY

Non-Western nations have long recognized the activity of the spirit world and its affect in the human realm. But recent trends in the Western world of recognizing the influence of the demonic on both individual and sociopolitical levels have led to a dramatic increase in what I am calling "holy warfare," similar to what some in varying ways call "spiritual warfare."

And while these terms are not found in Scripture, they are perhaps the best terms for what the apostle Paul speaks of in Eph. 6:12 when he says, "Our struggle is not against flesh and blood, but against . . . spiritual forces of evil in the heavenly realms." In numerous passages spanning both Old and New Testaments, we find a "struggle" or "war" going on in the spiritual realm. Sometimes the earthly manifestations are dramatic, at other times hardly noticeable.

Paul is clear that "the weapons we fight with . . . have divine power to demolish strongholds" and that the goal is to "take captive every thought to make it obedient to Christ" (2 Cor. 10:4-5). Our battle then is not simply spiritual; it is distinctly focused on Christ, so that all that is not under the Lord's authority will come to be. Such obedience and Christlikeness is what a life of holiness is all about. Our warfare then is not only spiritual but also distinctly holy.

THE NATURE OF HOLY WARFARE

By "holy warfare," then, I mean the overall conflict between the kingdom of God versus the kingdom of Satan and his legions of evil spirits. Since the matter is spiritual, prayer stands as the key instrument in our activity. In addition to prayer and the work of God, Scripture indicates that through sin and rebellion against God, humans and human society are under Satan's influence. The world, the flesh, and the devil then become almost inextricably intertwined. Thus, holy warfare involves all of the Christian life.

"Powers of darkness," a term paraphrased from Eph. 6, refers to spiritual beings of the demonic realm under Satan's control who oppose God, His purpose, and His people. "Cosmic powers" is also a term used widely in academic circles for spiritual beings (usually evil) in and above the human sphere, that is, on a higher, broader level than what normally affects individuals.

After years of study and experience in things related to holy warfare, I have often seen the need for clarification of what biblical texts actually say and what they do not say. A look at biblical texts in chapters 4 and 5 of this book shows that Scripture reveals quite a bit about how demonic spirits operate and how the people of God overcome them. Better clarification will then lead to a more biblically based theology and practical response.

I have also found that some very important and fundamentally biblical issues do not seem to be sufficiently recognized or practiced. Many who do engage in confronting the powers of darkness are heroic in prayer. Yet the Bible calls for an integrated response, involving all of life. I am convinced that those in the Wesleyan tradition have much to say on this topic, even if they may not realize it.

Holy Warfare Is Not an Option

Jesus died on the Cross to save us. But no one will get saved unless he or she personally appropriates the work of Christ. Also, at the Cross the devil was defeated and His power over us was broken. He is a defeated foe. But in the same way, unless we appropriate our victory over the devil, we will not necessarily experience it when we struggle with temptation, with church-related difficulties, or with people in bondage to sin.

Throughout Scripture every battle ever fought—whether by the armies of Israel, Jesus himself, or the Early Church—was won when the people of God believed and obeyed. *But the battles still had to be fought.* Furthermore, Scripture gives no indication that the battles would cease until Jesus' triumphant return. In fact, the New Testament consistently indicates that satanic activity will increase as we move toward the latter days leading to the Second Coming.

First Pet. 5:8 says, "The devil prowls around like a roaring lion looking for someone to devour." The next verse urges us to "resist him, standing firm in the faith" (v. 9). That is holy warfare. First John 5:19 tells us that "the whole world is under the control of the evil one." Though the devil is a defeated foe, he will not give up without a fight. And that same verse affirms, "We know that we are children of God." Recognizing our identity in Christ and exercising our delegated authority, we have the victory.

Rather than lament that the Christian life involves such resistance, remember that it is through this that God builds us, grows us, and leads us on in Christian perfection. God has in fact given us the task of prayer and witness that lead others "out of darkness into his wonderful light" (1 Pet. 2:9).

Pitfalls and the Needed Lifestyle

Two extremes to avoid are similar to those C. S. Lewis points out: "There are two equal and opposite errors into which our race can fall about the devils. One is to disbelieve in their existence. The other is to believe, and to feel an excessive and unhealthy interest in them. They themselves are equally pleased by both errors, and hail a materialist or a magician with the same delight."[4] Feeling an excessive interest in dark powers, one can engage in holy warfare to the extent of neglecting holiness in life. Focusing too much on the powers of darkness will also draw attention away from the worship and glorification of God. And it can lead us to look for the devil in every problem, no matter how human the cause. On the other hand, even though believing in the existence of demons, one can presume it unnecessary to engage in holy warfare. Or because Christ has won the victory on the Cross, one could ignore the vicious fight still being waged by our defeated foe. Both extremes miss the biblical mark. The apostle Paul is among our clearest biblical examples in that he lived a life of holiness and intimacy with God while at the same time continually confronting the powers of darkness as he spread the gospel message.

Sometimes those who confront the powers of darkness seem to overlook the importance of a life of holiness. As it is practiced, holy warfare can at times become reductionistic. We should take care that we don't expect prayers and proclamations to somehow evict demons and sweep people into the Church without realizing the need to live out Christian life and witness in the day-to-day grind.

This is precisely where the Wesleyan-Holiness tradition has an important place in the Christian Church's overall battle against evil. "[Wesley's] distinctive contribution was his conviction that true biblical Christianity finds its highest expression and ultimate test of authenticity in the practical and ethical experience of the individual Christian and only secondarily in doctrinal and propositional definition."[5] It is this emphasis of living out the Christian message, with a conscious view toward overcoming the powers of darkness, that is much needed in the Church's wrestling with the powers of darkness.

2

A Wesleyan Perspective

HOW DOES THE WHOLE IDEA of holy warfare, the confronting or wrestling with powers of darkness, fit into the Wesleyan-Holiness tradition? If Wesleyan-Holiness doctrine is truly biblical, holy warfare must have a place, for as we will see the New Testament example in more detail in chapter 5, wrestling with the powers of darkness is standard practice in the Christian life of the New Testament.

How then does wrestling with the powers of darkness fit into a Wesleyan perspective? I believe it is to be found in the power of the Holy Spirit and of love that overcomes evil. And it is in this very area that Wesleyans have much to offer to the Christian community with regard to holy warfare.

Serious scholarly investigation as to the nature of spiritual powers of evil (at least in the Western world) has received attention only during the latter half of the 20th century. Until then, little attention was paid, and "statements about the powers were either read as a confirmation of the conventional orthodox doctrine about angels and devils, or else they were seen as the last vestiges of an antiquated mythology."[1] In recent years many attempts have been made at interpreting the true nature of these powers and the appropriate response.

In the Wesleyan perspective we are drawn to issues of the grace of God; holiness; the cleansing, empowering work of the Spirit; and the culminating centrality of love. These will help define our approach to holy warfare.

GRACE

God is sovereign over all creation, including the powers of darkness. But does that mean that God in His sovereignty somehow wills evil upon His creation for some higher purpose? God obviously allows evil, and Scripture indicates that God brings disaster upon certain people for the purpose of punishing or correcting them (for a good purpose). But thinking of the Hitlers, the Stalins, the Idi Amins, and the Pol Pots of the world, does God actually will such atrocious attacks on innocent humanity? What does one say about persecution against Christians? Is it God's will for faithful believers to be disfranchised, imprisoned, or tortured to death? Conundrums regarding evil and the sovereignty of God bedevil those in traditions that do not recognize how God's creatures, both physical as well as spiritual, have free will within the sphere of His ultimate sovereignty. A strict Calvinistic interpretation of God's sovereignty disallows any contrary will or action, for such would be seen as a threat to that sovereignty. Gregory Boyd writes of this position, saying, "The hope that the New Testament offers is not the hope that God has a higher, all-encompassing plan that secretly governs every event, including the evil intentions of malicious angelic and human beings, and that somehow renders these evil wills 'good' at a higher level. . . . That supposition generates a truly hopeless situation."[2]

The whole of Scripture affirms the sovereignty of God while at the same time depicting a fallen creation in rebellion against Him. God's creation is both physical and spiritual. But just as human beings are given the free will to obey or disobey God, so also the same seems to be true with spiritual beings. (See, for example, Isa. 14:12-15; Ezek. 28:12-17; 2 Pet. 2:4; Jude 6; and Rev. 12:3-9.) Until the final judgment, God allows this rebellion to continue, both in the physical world and in the spiritual world.

Given that "the whole world is under the control of the evil one" (1 John 5:19), humanity would be incapable of goodness apart from the grace of God and would also be devoid of hope. The hope that grace gives us is life-encompassing. Grace enables salvation, living the Christian life, sanctification, all goodness that is enacted, even the very sustenance of life, not to mention the assurance of eternal life in the presence of God. Thus, as God's grace is essential to all things in life, it is naturally essential to overcoming the powers of darkness. Our victory is by grace, for "thanks be to God! He gives us the victory through our Lord Jesus Christ" (1 Cor. 15:57).

Receiving God's grace is always relational and never mechanical. Mildred Bangs Wynkoop states, "Grace is not an impersonal *power* or a *thing* to be received. It is God making himself available to us. It is the full measure of His redemptive love held out to us without reserve."[3] To experience grace, then, is not to get a mechanical blessing but to experience God himself in a personal way. Thus, in the context of holy warfare, it is not so important what we do or what procedures we enact. What is important is knowing who we are as children of God, maintaining a close, obedient relationship with God and acting on that rather than on any given methodology.

One thing is sure: the powers of darkness are no more powerful than God's grace, any more than we human beings are. Since God is omnipotent, we know that His grace is fully powerful to overcome these dark powers. It is our job to act upon it.

Will we fulfill our God-given role in appropriating His grace for victory here and now?

HOLINESS

Far from being merely one of God's attributes, holiness is the very essence of God's character. The repeated statement "Be holy, because I am holy" indicates God's desire, His expectation, that we share in His holiness. In the same way, "Wesley's overwhelming passion for his own life and for the lives of his followers was *holiness*. The whole of his preaching is directed toward the *goal of sanctification*."[4]

In the sanctification experience, the Holy Spirit cleanses the heart, ridding the believer of carnal bondages. The believer experiences victory over sin and empowerment for a way of life characterized by Spirit-filled living. With a pure heart of love for the Lord, the power of canceled sin is broken, and the believer is empowered to live worthily of God. "Two things then are permanent in the gift of the Holy Spirit," says E. Stanley Jones, "purity and power. Purity for myself and my own inner needs, and power to witness effectively to others."[5] In a life of holiness, the believer is empowered to witness with a Spirit-filled vibrancy, for that believer lives a Spirit-cleansed, Spirit-empowered life in the face of a sinful world.

Personal holiness shuts out the devil's work in one's own life, but personal holiness will not stop the devil from working in a fallen world. On the other hand, fighting the devil's work without living a life of holiness gives the devil a foothold (Eph. 4:27) and is a virtual setup for self-destruction. The apostle Paul lived a holy life but was engaged in considerable holy warfare.

Jesus calls us to "go into all the world" (Mark 16:15). The same Holy Spirit who sanctifies believers calls and empowers believers to go sanctify society. The aggregate sum of the carnal nature in unsanctified individuals is readily seen in society as a whole. Unfortunately, it is even seen in churches. Every large-scale revival has impacted the moral fabric of the Church and the surrounding society. But in daily life when there is no revival, are we content with personal piety when the society around us is on the road to hell?

Our holiness has always had a social dimension. Wesley emphasized it when he said that Christianity "is essentially a social religion . . . it cannot subsist at all, without society—without living and conversing with other men. . . . To turn this religion into a solitary one is to destroy it."[6] Wesleyans continue to emphasize it. But many of us live in societies that appear to be increasingly influenced by evil, if not outright demonic powers. The powers of darkness do not reason, negotiate, or repent. They deceive, steal, and destroy. To extend holiness from the personal into the social arena will require an awareness that demonic powers do influence people and events in our world.

Holy people are dangerous to the devil. People who faithfully live a life of holiness do not fall into the devil's snares. They lead others out of them. They live and love and pray the devil's work away. The light of the glory of God in their lives shines in the darkness as Jesus' did, and the darkness has not overcome it (see John 1:5). Holy people often don't know how dangerous they are to the devil. Because they don't know, they don't always exercise their authority over the powers of darkness. But that authority is ours in Christ, and Scripture shows us how to exercise it.

PERFECT LOVE AS A CENTRAL ISSUE IN WESLEYANISM

Throughout the New Testament love is the central issue in God's relationship with us and our relationships with one another. "God is love," says 1 John 4:16. "For God so loved the world that he gave his one and only Son," Jesus proclaimed in John 3:16. Characteristically, Jesus showed the disciples "the full extent of his love" (John 13:1) through action, whether healing, forgiving, washing feet, or dying on the Cross. "All men will know that you are my disciples, if you love one another," He asserted in John 13:35. Paul agrees, saying, "Over all these virtues put on love, which binds them all together in perfect unity" (Col. 3:14).

Likewise, according to John Wesley, "holiness, as well as grace, is defined in terms of love—so much so that it is virtually identified with love."[7] He also writes, "This is the sum of Christian perfection: It is all comprised in that one word, Love. The first branch of it is the love of God: And as he that loves God loves his brother also, it is inseparably connected with the second: 'thou shalt love thy neighbour as thyself:' Thou shalt love every man as thy own soul, as Christ loved us. 'On these two commandments hang all the Law and the Prophets:' These contain the whole of Christian perfection."[8]

W. T. Purkiser, Richard S. Taylor, and Willard H. Taylor point out that "loving is what holiness does. When it ceases to love, it ceases to exist, and shrinks into sterile moralism."[9] Love, to be genuine, must be expressed. It is not enough that a person merely believes in holiness, God's grace, and love. We must receive God's holiness, grace, and love through faith and then act on them to the point of a personally transforming experience.

THE RESPONSE OF LOVE:
TWO FACETS OF HOLY WARFARE

When we love God and His kingdom, we desire to see the Kingdom expand. God's love in turn compels us to love people, and we desire for them to know God. We develop a passion to see people enter the Kingdom. Satan is maliciously opposed to lost people knowing God and to those who know God living victoriously. In the face of this opposition, our love must be expressive and deliberate. How, then, do we act out love for God and love for people?

The response of love is comprised of the two most important facets of holy warfare: prayer and lifestyle.

Prayer: Love on Its Knees

Dick Eastman, in a book by the same title, refers to intercession as "love on its knees." "The fashioning of an intercessor, then, begins not so much with a burden to pray as with a burden to love—a burden that leads the intercessor ultimately to intense sessions of compassionate prayer."[10] Godly motivation to pray has nothing to do with, even shuns, spiritual pride, self-serving attitudes, or any Ramboesque shoot-em-up ambitions to attack the enemy. Without love, a person will not pray long.

Perhaps you know someone who regularly prays for hours. People such as this pray far beyond what most believers muster themselves to do, and they love it. Anyone who prays seriously and passionately soon finds that focused, intense, breakthrough prayer is hard work. Some ask if this motivation (or calling) is founded on some spiritual gift. Of all the gifts that Paul lists, the one that such people tend to have in common is the gift of mercy (Rom. 12:8). While the connection is inconclusive, it does reinforce the idea that loving, caring about, and feeling compassion for people is a central motivating factor in a person's prayer life. And whether or not we have this gift, we are still called to love—and love prays.

If you love a person, you'll pray for him or her. If you love your family, friends, and colleagues, you'll pray for them. If you love your church, you'll pray for them (especially your pastor!). If you love your community, you'll pray for them. If you love your nation, you'll pray for your nation.

Scripture is replete with passages that demonstrate how God acts in response to prayer. Ps. 141:2 symbolically likens prayer to incense before God. Rev. 5:8 depicts incense as "the prayers of the saints." Then Rev. 8:3-5 symbolizes this prayer dramatically answered. Moses, Samuel, David, Daniel, Jesus, and Paul provide strong examples of prayer and answered prayer. We are further exhorted many times to pray. To cite just a few cases, Matt. 9:38 tells us to "ask the Lord of the harvest, therefore, to send out workers." Mark 9:28-29 informs us that some evil spirits "come out only by prayer." Luke 18:1 exhorts us to "always pray and not give up." James 5:16 encourages, "The prayer of a righteous man is powerful and effective."

God in His sovereignty has obviously chosen to act in concert with the prayers of His people. Were He not to operate this way, we would certainly fall into spiritual slumber. The sum weight of Scripture shows that God's way is to work through human vessels. Sovereign acts apart from any human participation are more the exception than the rule.

Lifestyle: Love in Action

As God's love for us is seen by His grace, our love for God is expressed by a holy life. This is fundamental to any victory in one's personal life, within the Body of Christ, and in the world. A life of holiness separates us unto the Lord, but that separation is from sin in our own life and in the world—not a separation from society itself.

Jesus was quite clear about the centrality of love in any kind of effective witness when He said, "By this all men will know that you are my disciples, if you love one another" (John 13:35). Our effectiveness in witness will rise only as high as its consistency with our love. Heart purity, love, and forgiveness are critical in overcoming the influences of dark powers. If Christians make a bad name for themselves, how can they possibly hope to influence a society whose eyes are blind? But if Christians earn a reputation of love, no matter what is said or done to them, they will ultimately overcome. Such was the experience of the persecuted Church under imperial Rome and countless oppressive regimes since then. Despite victory, the price is sometimes high. Will we pay it?

Whether this lifestyle of love is heroic or commonplace, to consistently live such a life we need the infilling of the Holy Spirit. Without this, believers will try their best but eventually get worn down. It is a life dependent on the Lord and His grace. The infilling of the Spirit not only enables us to live this way but also draws others to Christ in us. The Holy Spirit is the contagion that undermines the devil's undermining to lead others out of darkness into light.

This life of love calls us to holy warfare by confronting the powers of darkness with an opposite spirit. Satan deceives; a life of love affirms God's truth. Satan aggravates and tears apart human relations; a life of love forgives, reconciles, and restores relations. Satan entices people, and collectively societies, down the path of moral degradation; a life of love stands up against immorality and aligns itself with Scripture where Scripture is clear. Satan breeds hate and upheaval; a life of love breeds peace. Satan robs, injures, deprives, and destroys; a life of love gives, heals, provides, and rebuilds. Satan oppresses and depresses; a life of love uplifts and encourages. Satan spews despair; a life of love heralds hope.

The New Testament never exalts any kind of prayer strategies over the basics of living like followers of Christ, evangelizing and caring for a lost, hurting world and taking a stand whenever necessary. Living a holy life, standing for what is right, caring for the poor and suffering are like prayer in action and all part of the war on evil.

3

How Do We Know What We Think We Know?

WITH SOME THINGS IN LIFE we might have total certainty, but with other things we might assume more certainty than is warranted, or we may admit we don't know all there is to know. The spiritual realm has a lot of room for "I don't know."

So how do we know what we think we know? We might begin dealing with this question, known as "epistemology," by recognizing the worldview out of which we come, then by establishing our interpretive approach, from which everything else is defined. In light of that, we interpret both Scripture and the experiences we encounter. None of us is a blank sheet. Interpretation of Scripture and our experience is critical to attaining usefulness and effectiveness in biblically based holy warfare.

WORLDVIEW AS BACKGROUND

"Worldview" is essentially a person's or society's basic assumptions about reality, which give rise to beliefs and behavior. Few people ever seriously examine their own worldview, for these assumptions are largely taken for granted and assumed to be correct. Since they generally go unexamined, people may have no idea as to how much or why their views are so different from others'. Anthropologist Paul Hiebert remarks, "People believe that the world really is the way they see it. Rarely are they aware of the fact that the way they see it is molded by their world view."[1] For example, I had a European teaching colleague who grew up with empirical science answering all his questions about the world. To him, anything spiritual was theoretical and either a ritualistic part of society or pure imagination. I have also had repeated contact with pastors and evangelists from Asian and African nations who grew up with shamanism and witchcraft. To some of them, anything scientific was a frail attempt at describing what was obviously a spiritual issue at heart.

Charles Kraft points out that two basic types of assumptions are made in worldview. One is "the way things are," including beliefs about God, the universe and the world around us, as well as the nature of humans and human life. The other is "values," assumptions that provide the bases for judgments concerning what is good and bad in aesthetics, ethics, economics, human character, and relationships.[2]

In the context of dark powers, our own worldview has much to do in deciding what the powers really are and what to do about them—whether they are spiritual entities in themselves or culturally related manifestations. Perhaps the most critical area of worldview in this context is our perception of activity in the spiritual realm as it touches upon the things of this world.

THE "EXCLUDED MIDDLE"

The African came to the missionary seeking help from affliction by demons, for he had heard about the power of Jesus.

But instead of taking authority over the powers of darkness in the name of Jesus, the missionary told the African not to be superstitious and to just trust the Lord who saved him from his sins. The man went back to his village and eventually sought help from the local witch doctor, whom he knew would directly address his problem.

The biblical writers lived in a world that understood "heaven" on three levels, which is to say, they described spiritual realities in their own language and conceptions, just as we do every day. The "first heaven" was the sky, the clouds, the sun, and the stars. "The heavens declare the glory of God; the skies proclaim the work of his hands," says Ps. 19:1. The "third heaven" was the dwelling place of God, as Paul speaks of in 2 Cor. 12:2. Evil spirits, separated from God by their uncleanness, do not come to the throne room as depicted in Rev. 4 and 5. Where, then, did the biblical writers place spirit activity, whether of angels or of demons? Where does the "holy war" go on? Rev. 14:6 speaks of the *mezzouranos,* the "middle heaven" (often rendered "midair") through which an angel was flying. This is likely the meaning of Rev. 12:7, which says, "there was war in heaven." Thus we see the dwelling place of God, of spirit activity, and of humans. Scripture regularly depicts unseen spiritual beings, both angelic and demonic, who are active on this earth. They occupy what Paul Hiebert calls the "middle zone"[3] or what theologian Gregory A. Boyd terms "the world in between" us and God.[4] The point is not to identify some stratospheric location of presumed spirits but to recognize, as the Bible does, that unseen spirits are active in this present, physical world.

Since the 17th and 18th centuries, particularly from the time of the Enlightenment, when rationalism replaced traditional ideas of society and religion, Westerners increasingly accepted a science and a view of the world based on materialistic naturalism. What happened was that things of the empirical

world—that which one could see, touch, and experience—
were understood through science. The nonmaterial, other-
worldly things were left to religion. As scientific knowledge
grew and became increasingly prominent, acceptance of unseen, supernatural phenomena related to our life on earth de-
creased. Thus, many denied the existence of spirits or the possibility of miracles. While most Bible-believing Christians
affirmed the existence of spirits and the possibility of miracles,
many were no longer able to discern the existence or activity of
spirits or expect the occurrence of miracles.

Following this, fear of evil spirits, curses, and so on has often been met with the assertion that it is superstitious rather
than with the assertion of Christ's power over the problem,
whatever its true nature. Not knowing how to deal with the
subject, believers may claim victory in Christ without pragmat-
ically applying it or working it out in tough situations.

The point is this: though there is now a resurgence of interest
in the supernatural, Westerners, including Christians, have for a
long time excluded this "middle zone" from their thinking.
Judging by the world's circumstances, both on the world scene
and in our local churches, it would seem that the powers of
darkness have taken advantage of their being denied or ignored.
It is time to see the spiritual world as the Bible depicts it, not as
our Western, scientific way of thinking depicts it, and to exercise
our authority and victory in Christ over the spirits that be.

With a subject as elusive as spiritual powers, objectivity is
difficult. This makes awareness of our interpretive approach
vitally important.

INTERPRETIVE APPROACHES

Have you tried to convince people of something and felt as
though you were talking right past them? One reason might
have been that individuals hold different interpretive ap-

proaches. We can find four general approaches, all of which are observable among people who engage in confrontation of evil powers. In each may be found both extreme and moderate positions. In identifying these positions, I am indebted to Hiebert's foundational work.[5]

While comparing these four general positions, it is helpful to remember that people who hold to any one do so largely because of what they have been taught to believe all their lives. They also do so (or they change) because of their experiences (or lack of them) and how they choose to deal with these experiences. Where do you find yourself with each of these four areas? Where do others find you?

Idealist

For the idealist, reality exists in the mind. For some Hindus, this means that the world is an illusion. But in a more common and moderate sense, it means we interpret the world according to what is in our minds. Our ideals (in our minds) are what really matter, "the way things are supposed to be" (whether or not they really are), and are the dominant force in our interpretations of Scripture and of our experience.

Related to powers of darkness, a person taking this position might say, "I believe spirits cause these problems; therefore, a spirit is causing *this* problem." Or perhaps, "I do not believe spirits cause these problems; therefore, spirits have nothing to do with *this* problem."

Naive Realist

For the naive realist, reality can be known exactly as it is. Accurate judgments can be made without bias. The reality of anything equals our interpretation of it. Thus, we can interpret Scripture, or anything for that matter, exactly as it was intended to be known, and experiences can be understood exactly as they really are. Any disagreement is simply wrong.

Related to powers of darkness, a person taking this position might say, "Spirits are behind problems—I am simply making a correct observation." Or perhaps, "Spirits are not behind problems—I am simply making a correct observation."

Critical Realist

For the critical realist, reality can be known, but it cannot necessarily be known for certain all the time. We may have high or even total certainty about Scripture or experience. But our knowledge is more indicative of our understanding of what we encounter than of the ultimate reality itself. We are relatively open to correction, new discoveries, and improvement.

Related to powers of darkness, a person taking this position might say, "A spirit may or may not be behind a given problem. We'll have to discern to the best of our ability."

Instrumentalist

An instrumentalist is not terribly concerned with truth or with reality vs. illusion. Truth, and therefore doctrine and scriptural interpretation, is of secondary importance. What's important is whether something works. Choices of action are based on whether they appear effective in the task or are accepted by others.

Related to powers of darkness, a person taking this position might say, "I don't know whether any spirit is related to this problem and if what I'm doing is right. I'll just do whatever works."

SCRIPTURAL INTERPRETATION

When Paul said, "Our struggle is not against flesh and blood" (Eph. 6:12), what did he mean? In looking at the biblical text, we should remember that throughout the history of biblical hermeneutics, debates on textual interpretation have revolved around three areas: the original author and context, the text itself, and the reader. An awareness of these three areas is essential to good interpretation.

First, we must have some knowledge of the author and the author's purpose in writing. We should also know about the geographical, historical, and social context in which the author wrote. From these items we may more closely know the author's intended meaning. Second, study of the text requires us to pay attention to the meaning, use, and grammar of the words themselves. We must be aware of the text's genre, since slightly different exegetical principles apply to different genre. Is it narrative, poetry, wisdom, prophecy, apocalyptic, parable, or epistle?[6] Third, worldview and interpretive approaches are essentially the issues to be dealt with. We should be careful of prejudicial readings of the text, something that may happen more easily than we admit. Presuppositions may be unavoidable but need to be identified, since they influence our interpretation.

From all this it appears evident that an accurate, viable textual interpretation comes best from the critical realist approach as described above. It is the only approach that recognizes both our abilities and limitations in interpreting reality while avoiding the instrumentalist danger of simply doing whatever works.

EXPERIENTIAL INTERPRETATION

My wife and I planted a church in Japan aimed at bar hostesses and Japanese mafia. Before long, backbiting, manipulating, deceit, and physical violence left the church in shambles both spiritually and physically. Eventually the building was torched by an arsonist. What were we to make of all this? Where did the carnal, human side end and the sinister dark force of evil begin? Or vice versa?

It is important that we interpret experiences much as we interpret the Bible. This parallel is more than coincidental, for the biblical text itself was written out of experiences with God. Parallel to textual interpretation, we have the persons (or spirits) involved, the experience itself, and the observer. And as with the biblical text, we should maintain a critical realist approach. Interpreting the experience is done first by applying the Bible and second by comparing other experiences. While experience imparts insight to one's reading of Scripture, we must take care to interpret events through Scripture and to avoid interpreting Scripture through events.

Whenever hearing reports, we must consider the integrity of what is claimed as well as that of the individual making it. When you hear that a demon is the main reason for a person's illness, do you accept it without question? Do you completely disregard such a notion? Hopefully neither. You may discover a bunch of malarkey, or you may discover how evil spirits sometimes afflict humans, just as the Spirit of God heals humans.

In this area look for conflict against (or between) Christians; discernible evil in cultural elements themselves; evil in the church; spiritual influence over individuals, groups, social systems, or political structures; and people's worship of pagan religions that may influence spirits.

KEEPING THE FOUR FACTORS IN BALANCE

We have looked at four factors involved in a clear understanding: worldview (especially an awareness of the "middle zone"), interpretive approach, Scripture, and experience. It is important to keep these factors in proper balance, not focusing on one to the ignorance of others. To make this point, I will observe the possible consequences of overemphasis and underemphasis in each area.

Overemphasis on worldview would make us so analytical we would never look forward. This could also lead to a deterministic approach (such that everything we do results from our worldview). *Underemphasis* would leave us ignorant of what shapes our assumptions and interpretation so that we enter a situation presumptuously. This would in turn influence what kind of interpretive approach we choose, which would probably be anything but critical realistic.

Overemphasis on the interpretive approach again would make us so analytical we would have little room left for application or action. *Underemphasis on the interpretive approach* allows us to easily fall into presumption and errors stemming from idealism, naive realism, or instrumentalism. This in turn may result in misinterpretation of Scripture and ineffective or misconstrued application and action.

"Overemphasis" of Scripture is not really possible. However, if we ignore all else, we may have great Bible studies but fail to apply the text to what is actually happening around us. This would be somewhat like giving a fire prevention lecture in a building that is burning down. *Underemphasis of Scripture* would take interpretation of experience as being primary, which it is not. Scripture is. This approach "runs ahead" and thus "does not have God" (2 John 9). A practitioner who takes a few texts or proof texts and moves into action may move too quickly or too far. The results can and do range from ineffectual to disastrous.

Overemphasis of experience encourages countless stories but neglects biblical foundations and parameters for any reasonable assessment. *Underemphasis of experience* may limit the work of God in holy warfare to ages past, leaving the Christian ineffectual in the face of Satan's present activity.

THE ROLE OF THE HOLY SPIRIT

To whatever extent we may apply any methodology, we must always give a place to discernment through the inspiration of the Holy Spirit. Through whatever form of spiritual insight, the Holy Spirit will guide us. Yet in an effort to avoid extremes or abuses, inspiration by the Spirit likewise must be handled with a critical realist approach and be subject to the written Word of God.

In the final analysis, how do we know if we are right? The passage of time and what it brings are our surest confirmation.

4

An Old Testament View of Spiritual Confrontation

ANYTHING WE CLAIM TO KNOW about the spirit world and any pursuit of holy warfare must be firmly grounded on an understanding of the biblical text. The Bible tells us that God is universal, that He is all-powerful and in all places at once. The enemy, Satan, is a created being with an army of created beings who can thus be in only one place at one time. Then how can spiritual beings in a spiritual world influence physical people in a physical world? We will find that if these powers are active in any certain place, it is because they are active among the *people* of that place. We should concern ourselves, therefore, with questions on the relationship between demonic powers and humans.

In each passage we face the hermeneutical question of how to read the text. Does it describe only the people's perceptions? Or does it depict the true reality from God's perspective? As we take a critical realist approach while acknowledging that spirits do exist and are somehow active in this world, the goal will be to discern spiritual realities as they are expressed or implied in the texts.

Some textual references will not be included. For example, throughout the Old Testament, "high places" are places of spiritual significance and may be important in the influence of demonic powers on spiritists, besides being places where God's people prayed. For example, see Num. 22:41; Deut. 12:2; 1 Sam. 9:12-14; 10:5; and 1 Kings 3:2-4. I will not include these in my survey of texts, nor will I include every Old and New Testament reference to demonic activity or expulsion of demons, for there are far too many. I will purposely limit this examination to what relates to the powers of darkness, particularly as they influence people and societies.

In surveying Old Testament texts, we will primarily observe the powers of darkness as revealed through narratives. We should not forget that the worldview of the Hebrew people accepted the supernatural manifestations described, nor should we forget that the writers were inspired by the Holy Spirit.

Let us attempt to see as the Old Testament writers may have, by going back and encountering Yahweh in the face of the Gentile people and their gods.

Significant Texts Related to Powers of Darkness

Common biblical translations have not been completed with an eye to the specific issue of spiritual powers. Thus, to expedite the full impact of key words and concepts, I will offer my own translation of each text. For this purpose I will deliberately lean toward a more literal rendering, with alternate terms provided as needed.

When reading our Old Testaments, we read "LORD" in capital and small capital letters, signifying the name "Yahweh," the Hebrew name for God. I will use this name "Yahweh" in an attempt to bring out the unique and specific sense of the personal nature of God as the Hebrew people knew Him.

Gen. 6:2-4—Wickedness Before the Flood

The sons of God [or sons of gods] saw that the daughters of men were beautiful, and they took wives for themselves from whomever they chose. Then Yahweh said, "My Spirit will not contend with man forever, for he is mortal; his days will be a hundred and twenty years."

The Nephilim were on the earth in those days—and also afterward—when the sons of God went to the daughters of men and bore [children] to them. They were the mighty men of old, men of renown *(Gen. 6:2-4)*.

The term "sons of God" can also be translated "sons of gods." Were they angels, as many presume to be their identity in Job 1:6? Were they demons? Were they references to pagan myth? Or were they humans of high social or spiritual standing? Their identity is so debated as to be outside the scope of the present study. The Nephilim are also a mystery. If they are the same Nephilim as recorded in Num. 13:33, what does that say of the Flood narrative in between these references? Could this be a more general term referring to great warriors rather than some kind of hybrid race? Taking the position that these mysterious occurrences were in some way factual compels us to acknowledge the great mystery of what we face and the seriousness with which we must approach it.

Exod. 17:8-16—Battle with the Amalekites

As long as Moses held up his hands, the Israelites prevailed, but whenever he lowered his hands, the Amalekites prevailed *(Exod. 17:11)*.

Raised hands in the Hebrew context implies prayer or exercising God's authority, and it cannot be denied that the raising of Moses' hands and staff brought about Israel's victory by God's power. The text strongly implies that power resides first of all in the spiritual dimension and that an unseen battle was raging over the human warriors. The text also demonstrates how the human leader, Moses, had everything to do with empowering the forces on his side. The text is an unequivocal witness of the direct connection between spiritual and human activity.

Deut. 32:17—The Song of Moses

They sacrificed to demons, which are not God—gods they had not known, that recently appeared, that your fathers did not fear *(Deut. 32:17)*.

The Old Testament is replete with references to pagan gods and the sacrifices given to them. This passage is significant in that it clearly identifies the "gods" as demons. The same verse immediately continues with three phrases that refer to them as gods. This clearly tells us that Scripture equates the term "god" or "gods" with demons (except, of course, in cases in which humans declare themselves gods). Thus, when we read of the "gods" of certain people, we know that these are in fact demons. See also Ps. 106:36-38.

1 Sam. 5:2-4—The Philistines Capture the Ark of God

Then they carried the ark of God into Dagon's temple and set it beside Dagon. When the Ashdodites rose early the next day, there was Dagon, fallen on his face on the ground before the ark of Yahweh! They took Dagon and put him back in his place. But they rose the next morning, and there was Dagon, fallen on his face on the ground before the ark of Yahweh! The head of Dagon and both palms were broken off on the threshold; only Dagon's body remained *(1 Sam. 5:2-4)*.

The Philistines brought their war trophy, the ark of Yahweh, into the very seat of power of their god (demon) Dagon, perhaps to include Yahweh in their pantheon, perhaps to subordinate Him to Dagon. Their miscalculation left their idol broken apart and the people covered with tumors (see v. 6). Unlike Moses and the battle with the Amalekites, this text shows a spiritual confrontation devoid of any human involvement. Unlike their local god, Yahweh proved to be universal, powerful in any place or circumstance. No idol or demon can stand in His presence.

1 Kings 20:23—Israel Fights Aram

The officials of the king of Aram advised him, "Their gods are gods of the hills; that is why they were stronger than we. But if we fight them on the plains, surely we will be stronger than they" *(1 Kings 20:23).*

The statement from the king's officials obviously exhibits a territorial mentality regarding spirits, but its source is a group of pagans. So we must ask whether this statement reflects merely their perception of the spirit world or they actually know in some factual way that this is how spirits operate. The point of the story is once again Yahweh's demonstration that unlike the other gods, He is not bound by geography or topography but is universal, and His power is unlimited (see vv. 28-29). It seems that certain people groups so identified themselves and their territory with their gods that it was necessary for Yahweh to demonstrate and proclaim over and over that He was universal.

2 Kings 3:26-27—Battle with the Moabites

When the king of Moab saw that the battle prevailed against him, he took with him seven hundred swordsmen to break through to the king of Edom, but they could not. Then he took his firstborn son, who was to succeed him as king, and offered him as a burnt offering on the wall. Great wrath came against Israel, so they withdrew from him and returned to their own land *(2 Kings 3:26-27).*

The object of King Mesha's sacrifice finds no other explanation than Moab's national god, Chemosh. And the Old Testament bears out that Chemosh was the god of the Moabites and of no one else. By biblical definition, Chemosh is an evil spirit, and in eight places throughout the Old Testament it is mentioned by name as being detestable to Yahweh and headed along with the Moabites for destruction. The only explanation of "Great wrath came against Israel" that avoids manipulating the text is that the demonic spirit Chemosh acknowledged Mesha's greatest possible sacrifice of appeasement and petition and responded by unleashing a fury of tumult against the army of Israel, whether by directly causing panic upon Israel or by somehow empowering the Moabite army. Commentator John Gray agrees that "nothing was more natural than that Chemosh should be considered effective in his own land, especially after the supreme sacrifice by Mesha."[1] We have here a demon particular to the Moabite people, who exercised great power in his own land.

2 Kings 17:25-33—Samaria Resettled

When they first lived there, they did not worship Yahweh, so He sent lions among them, which killed some of them. So they reported to the king of Assyria: "The people you deported and resettled in the towns of Samaria do not know the requirements of the god of that land, and he has sent lions among them, which are killing them off because the people do not know the requirements of the god of the land."

Then the king of Assyria ordered: "Send back there one of the priests you exiled from there to go back to live there and teach them the requirements of the god of the land." So one of the priests who had been exiled from Samaria came and lived in Bethel and taught them how to worship Yahweh.

But they were nations [people groups] that made national [people group] gods and set them up in the shrines that the Samaritan nation [people] had made, every nation [people group] in the towns in which they lived. The men from Babylon made Succoth-Benoth, the men from Cuth made Nergal, and the men from Hamath made Ashima; the Avvites made Nibhaz and Tartak, and the Sepharvites burned their children in the fire to Adrammelech and Anammelech, the gods of Sepharvaim. . . . They worshiped Yahweh, but they also served their own gods as was the custom of the nations [people] from which they had been exiled *(2 Kings 17:25-33)*.

Of all Old Testament texts, this is the most lengthy and detailed treatment of how "gods" are related to people groups and their territories. Somewhat surprisingly, Yahweh is depicted almost as if He were a territorial god who destroys those who don't worship Him in His designated land. This may be explained in that Yahweh formed Israel, repeatedly called them "my people," and set their political boundaries. This text elucidates the tensions of Yahweh's universality and particularity, which was in effect until Christ's death and resurrection. Yet even still Yahweh maintains some particularity in His relationship to Israel (e.g., Rom. 10—11) and to Jerusalem (e.g., Rev. 21). In this text, as well as in the New Testament, His particularity is grounded primarily on Israel as the chosen people and by extension on the land designated to them.

Verses 29-33 show the other side. Though different people groups were taken from their own native lands and resettled in Samaria, they brought their gods with them. Each god is listed by name as relating specifically to each people group.[2]

2 Chron. 25:14-15—Amaziah After a Battle Victory

Now after he returned from slaughtering the Edomites, he brought back the gods of the people of Seir and set them up as his gods, bowed down before them, and made sacrifices to them. And the anger of Yahweh burned against Amaziah, and He sent a prophet to him, who said, "Why have you sought the gods of the people which could not save their own people from your hand?" *(2 Chron. 25:14-15).*

Raymond Dillard explains Amaziah's action, saying, "Not only did the royal deity assist the king in his battles, but also the deities of the opposing nation were often described as abandoning their people and coming to the aid of the attacking force." He rightly speculates that "Amaziah's homage to these deities may have represented his own gratitude that they had helped him."[3]

This is among the texts most clearly linking demonic spirits to people groups. That he apparently brought back idols of two or more gods implies that a people group may have a multiplicity of demons over them. Subsequent to this, Yahweh himself, through a prophet, acknowledged that these gods were indeed the gods of these particular people (not to mention that they were no match for the power of Yahweh).

2 Chron. 28:23—Ahaz in Distress

He sacrificed to the gods of Damascus who had defeated him, saying, "Since the gods of the kings of Aram help them, I will sacrifice to them so they will help me." But they were the stumbling of him and all of Israel *(2 Chron. 28:23).*

Here is a case very similar to the previous one, only that Ahaz was on the losing side. And just as before, we see numerous gods over the same people. That certain gods and groups of gods are over certain people groups is by now commonplace in the Old Testament. The significant point here is that grammatically the force that defeated him was not Damascus or the army of Aram but the *gods* of Damascus. Ahaz, as well as the author of Chronicles, attributed the battle loss not just to a superior army but, more prominently, to the gods of those people. Ahaz's mistake was in seeking the power of those spirits rather than repenting before Yahweh.

That the spirits caused all Israel to stumble indicates the social force they were able to generate: the attitude and values of the people were literally turned away from God.

Job 1:6-12; 2:6—Satan Asking to Afflict Job

The day came when the sons of God came to present themselves before Yahweh, and Satan also came among them. Yahweh said to Satan, "Where have you come from?"

Satan answered Yahweh, saying, "From roaming through the earth and going to and fro."

Then Yahweh said to Satan, "Have you set your heart to my servant Job? There is no one like him on the earth, a blameless and upright man fearing God and shunning evil."

Satan answered Yahweh, saying, "Does Job fear God for nothing? Have you not put a hedge around him and around his household and around all that he has? You have blessed the work of his hands so that his flocks spread throughout the land. But stretch out your hand and touch [strike] all that he has; he will surely curse you to your face."

And Yahweh said to Satan, "Behold, all that he has is in your hands, but do not lay a hand on him." So Satan went out from the presence of Yahweh. . . .

Yahweh said to Satan, "Behold, he is in your hands, but spare his life" *(Job 1:6-12; 2:6).*

This is one of the first mentions of Satan by name in Scripture. He is a being under God's authority, yet in his wandering and in the taunting way he speaks to Yahweh, he exhibits a rebellious semi-independence. He is not one of the "sons of God," a cryptic usage of the phrase taken by most commentators here to mean the angelic host. Rather, he comes in addition to these angels. And instead of being a prosecutor who acts out God's will, he is clearly a source of evil at enmity with God and God's people. Though possessing great power, Satan is on the same general level as the other angelic beings, and as a created being he is not on God's level.

We see that God protects the righteous. But He is willing to let them be tested through affliction. God allows this affliction, but with a purpose and blessing in the end. It is actually Satan, not God, who does the afflicting, though the responsibility falls on Yahweh. (See Job 2:3. This may help explain Isa. 45:7 and Amos 3:6. Lam. 3:38-39 indicates the more common pattern than with Job, that affliction is because of human sin.) In this example with Job, we see how Satan is restrained like a dog on a long leash in the damage he is allowed to do in a given circumstance.

Isa. 24:21—Prophecy of the Devastation of the Earth

It will happen in that day, Yahweh will punish the army [literally, host] of the height in the heights and the kings of the earth on the earth *(Isa. 24:21)*.

In this apocalyptic prophecy, Yahweh will punish the "host," which is essentially a military term and often indicates a group of people organized for war. It is, of course, also used with reference to angels. As to which heaven is referred to is not indicated, but we do know there is war in "heaven" between God's and Satan's forces (Rev. 12:7). As indicated in chapter 3, Scripture describes the natural "heavens" (Ps. 19:1), the "third heaven" or "paradise" in Paul's experience (2 Cor. 12:2-4), presumably the dwelling place of God, and germane to this text, a "middle heaven" *(mesouranema)* wherein angels are apparently active (see Rev. 14:6). If the "middle heaven" is where angelic and demonic forces are active, then this passage may be telling us that demonic forces in the heavenlies will be punished.

Jer. 50:2—Prophecy Against Babylon

Declare among the nations and proclaim; lift up a banner and proclaim; do not conceal it, but say, "Babylon is captured; Bel is put to shame, Marduk is shattered" *(Jer. 50:2)*.

"Bel" ("Baal" in Hebrew) is the Babylonian term for "lord." It is used as "the title of the state-god of Babylon, Marduk."[4]

Again Hebrew parallelism speaks of the same entities in different, parallel phrases, essentially saying, "Babylon will fall along with its god." Marduk is acknowledged as the tutelary god of Babylon, in other words, the demon having authority over the nation. An implication that could be drawn is that when the nation falls, so does the demon—and perhaps vice versa. Here we see again the intimate connection between a nation and the demonic power over it.

Ezek. 28:1-19—Prophecy Against Tyre

> The word of Yahweh came to me saying, "Son of man, say to the leader [or ruler, prince] of Tyre." . . .
>
> The word of Yahweh came to me saying, "Son of man, take up a lament concerning the king of Tyre" *(Ezek. 28:1, 11).*

The bulk of this chapter is two laments directed at Tyre. The first, from verse 1, is directed at the leader, ruler, or prince, literally "the one in front." By the ensuing text we know this is an arrogant human ruler who will be brought down. Verse 11 directs the parallel lament at "the king of Tyre" and by the ensuing text clarifies not only that this is a different personage but also that this being is supernatural. This being was in the Garden of Eden and highly adorned (v. 13), the highest rank of angels (v. 14), corrupted by pride (vv. 15, 17), and expelled and thrown to the earth (vv. 16-17). Who could this refer to but Satan himself?

This chapter gives yet another elucidation of the spiritual power behind a human ruler.

Dan. 8:23-25—Daniel's Interpretation of a Vision

> In the latter part of their rule, when rebels have reached full measure, a king will arise, strong faced and skilled in intrigue. He will become mighty in strength, but not by his own power. He will cause extraordinary devastation and

will succeed in whatever he does. He will destroy mighty men and the holy people. By his cunning he will cause deceit to prosper by his hand, and he will magnify himself in his heart. He will destroy many while they feel secure, and he will even stand against the Prince of princes. Yet he will be broken, but not by human power *(Dan. 8:23-25).*

This prophecy sounds very much like Rev. 13 and 19. Given the total wickedness and distinctly supernatural abilities of this figure, this is surely a demonic power, if not Satan himself, working behind a person. In further affirmation of this, the text is careful to note that his final destruction will not be by human power. Note again the inherent ability of satanic forces to influence and manipulate the human sphere.

Dan. 10:13-20—Daniel's Prayer and Vision

The prince of the Kingdom of Persia withstood me twenty-one days. Then Michael, one of the chief princes, came to help me, because I had been left there with the kings of Persia. . . . Now I will return to fight against the prince of Persia, and when I go, the prince of Greece will come *(Dan. 10:13, 20).*

The text above is a classic in identifying the evil figures over distinct geopolitical spheres. The figures, both angelic and demonic, were clearly not human, yet the demonic figures seemed to dominate certain earthly nations, Persia and Greece. It is curious that the angelic being was left among the kings (plural) of Persia. This may have been a duo of human and spirit or a plurality of spirits under the authority of the "prince" of the Persian kingdom. Since the entire episode is of spirit beings in spiritual conflict, these "kings" were quite likely spirits under the "prince," the chief demon. Commentator C. F. Keil concludes that this prince of Persia was "the supernatural spiritual power standing behind the national gods, which we may properly call the guardian spirit of this kingdom."[5]

Noteworthy is the fact that had the angel not informed Daniel of what had happened in the spiritual realm, Daniel would have had no knowledge at all of the spiritual battle that had occurred. Daniel was not directing the spiritual battle. He was simply compelled to fast for three weeks. He was living a holy, prayerful life and had no idea how much his life impacted what happened in the spiritual realm.

SIGNIFICANT TEXTS RELATED TO HOLY WARFARE

Josh. 5:13-15—Joshua Meets the Angel

Now when Joshua was near Jericho, he lifted up his eyes, and behold, a man was standing in front of him with his drawn sword in his hand. Joshua went to him and asked him, "Are you for us or for our enemies?"

And he replied, "Neither, but as commander of the army of Yahweh, I have now come." Then Joshua fell on his face to the ground in reverence and asked him, "What does my Lord say to His servant?"

The commander of Yahweh's army replied, "Take off your sandals from your feet, for the place where you are standing is holy." And Joshua did so *(Josh. 5:13-15)*.

Joshua at first did not discern who this "man" was, but it could be none other than an angel. The angel made clear that neither Yahweh nor His angels were on Joshua's side or his enemies'. Realizing who this was, Joshua affirmed that he himself was on God's side.

The angel was in charge of Yahweh's army of angels, who do His bidding. Yahweh clearly works through angels, perhaps not unlike the way He works through His people in the physical world. As in Daniel 10, angels are depicted as engaging in warfare against the enemies of God. (Their other main roles in

Scripture are conveying messages to people [as in Luke 1:26 ff.] and worshiping God [as in Rev. 5:11 ff.].) While Yahweh is omnipresent, the angel and the angelic army are not. The angel's manifestation is very temporal, even visible to the human eye. The emphasis of taking one's shoes off on holy ground, that is, where the presence of Yahweh is (particularly here in the person of the angel) affirms that the participants and purpose of the upcoming battle are holy.

The narrative continues by telling how Joshua was told to do the seemingly ridiculous act of marching around the city and blowing trumpets on seven consecutive days. Then on the final day after the people marched seven times around, blowing trumpets and shouting, God caused Jericho's walls to collapse, though the text does not reveal the invisible angelic versus demonic activity. The important thing is obedience to God.

Judg. 7:19-22—Gideon Defeats the Midianites

[Gideon and the three hundred men] blew the trumpets and smashed the jars. They grasped the torches in their left hands and the trumpets in their right hands to blow, and they shouted, "A sword for Yahweh and for Gideon!" And while each held his position around the camp, all the camp ran, crying out as they fled.

When they sounded the three hundred trumpets, Yahweh caused the sword of each to turn against the other, even throughout the camp, and the army fled (*Judg. 7:19-22*).

Similar to Joshua's orders at Jericho, Gideon and his men were told to do something that from the human point of view seemed ridiculous. Obedience brought Yahweh's response and a great victory. Note that "each held his position." The men stood still, not even moving. God was the one who did the fighting by confusing the enemy and causing them to destroy themselves.

2 Kings 6:15-18—Elisha at Dothan

When the servant of the man of God rose and went out early the next morning, behold, an army with horses and chariots was surrounding the city. And the servant asked him, "Oh, my lord, what shall we do?"

And he answered, "Don't be afraid, for those who are with us are more than those who are with them."

And Elisha prayed, saying, "O Yahweh, open his eyes so he may see." Then Yahweh opened the servant's eyes, and he looked, and behold, the hills were full of horses and chariots of fire all around Elisha.

As the enemy came down toward him, Elisha prayed to Yahweh, saying, "Strike these people with blindness." So He struck them with blindness, as Elisha had requested *(2 Kings 6:15-18).*

Elisha exhibited an unquestioning faith, or knowledge, that Yahweh was present to protect and fight for His people. Physical eyes could not see the spiritual realm. When God opened the servant's eyes, he saw the overwhelming power of God there to guard him. God's angelic army fully took on anthropomorphic imagery, even down to riding on horses and chariots. While the enemy surrounded the men of God, the army of God surrounded the enemy.

2 Kings 19:35—The Angel of Yahweh Annihilates the Assyrian Camp

That night the angel of Yahweh went out and killed one hundred eighty-five thousand in the camp of the Assyrians *(2 Kings 19:35).*

In the face of Sennacherib's arrogant threats against Hezekiah and Jerusalem, Yahweh showed His omnipotent power again through "the angel of Yahweh." Whether the angel singularly enacted God's power or acted as head of the angelic army as elsewhere is not revealed. This is one case in which an angel acted without any visible connection to human activity or the beseeching of God.

1 Chron. 14:14-16—David Defeats the Philistines

David inquired of God again, and God answered him, "Do not go up after them. Circle around them and attack them in front of the balsam trees. And it will be as you hear the sound of marching in the tops of the balsam trees, then move out to battle, because God has gone out in front of you to strike the army of the Philistines." So David did just as God commanded him, and they struck down the army of the Philistines, from Gibeon even to Gezer *(1 Chron. 14:14-16)*.

Earlier in verse 10 David inquired whether the battle should be fought at all, for if God did not want a particular battle fought, it should not be fought.

Regardless of how David might have planned to attack, God gave explicit directions on how to battle the enemy. By the sound of marching in the treetops, God gave a sign of His presence, a clear signal that the army of Yahweh was present and working on behalf of David and his army. We see here the importance of praying before any action is taken and then following in full obedience. Doing as God commanded, David won a great victory.

2 Chron. 20:15-23—Jehoshaphat Defeats Moab and Ammon

"Do not be afraid or discouraged because of this vast army. For the battle is not yours, but God's." . . .

[Jehoshaphat] appointed those singing to Yahweh and those praising Him for the splendor of his holiness as they went out before the ones in the army, saying, "Give thanks to Yahweh, for His love is forever."

As they began to sing and praise, Yahweh set ambushes against the sons of Ammon and Moab and Mount Seir who were invading Judah, and they were struck down. . . . They helped to destroy one another *(2 Chron. 20:15, 21-23)*.

God encouraged His people, affirming that the battle was His, thus His people needed not worry. Those praising did not simply accompany the army—they were in front, in a place of prime importance, if not danger. No other text so vividly demonstrates the power of praise and worship in holy warfare. Praise to God literally called forth His presence and power.

Exactly who the ambushes consisted of, angelic activity or God's directives on human soldiers, is unclear. But the term used, *mearbim,* is consistently used elsewhere to indicate humans. It is common for God to use people as He wills to accomplish His plan.

Again God's people did no physical fighting, but God put the opposing forces into confusion and they destroyed themselves.

Summary of Old Testament Texts

At this point it appears that nations or people groups may, through their own idol worship, be highly influenced by evil spirits carrying out Satan's intent. We find no biblical texts to deny the possibility. Satan's intent is obviously opposing and afflicting God's people.

Throughout the Old Testament the understanding that each people had their own god (spirit) was undisputed. Everyone, including the biblical writers and the people of the surrounding nations, understood and accepted this notion. When we read the Old Testament in an English translation, "Yahweh" is translated "the LORD," which to most of us bears an understood universal authority—Lord of the universe. But when the ancients spoke of Yahweh, it was clearly the God of Israel. With these ubiquitous assumptions of the linkage of gods to people groups or nations, the point the Old Testament hammers over and over is that Yahweh is more than just the "god" of the Israelite people. He alone is universal and over all other gods. The actual existence of these gods (in reality evil spirits) is never denied, nor is their association with individuals or people groups. The point is that Yahweh is sovereign over them, which is to say He is sovereign over every spirit, angelic or demonic—a consistent message that continues through the New Testament.

Military conflicts repeatedly convey the principle that behind a physical encounter is a spiritual dimension. The ancients clearly exhibited the concept that in warfare the strength of a people's gods made a critical difference in who won the battle. Some nations (e.g., Assyria, Babylon, and Egypt) were definitely stronger than others. Though Yahweh was stronger than all the demonic powers of Israel's enemies combined, this did not ensure that Israel won its battles. Whether or not Israel won a battle depended entirely on their faithful obedience to Yahweh.

The battles fought were ultimately God's, not the people's. And no two battles were the same. Thus, Israel's main responsibility was not attacking the enemy but beseeching God regarding the enemy. As God drew people into His battles, we find that angels were His representatives who did His work in coordination with people in the earthly realm. As God fought the battles, He often caused the enemy to be confused and to destroy itself. Whenever facing a confrontation, God's people had to act in total obedience, even if didn't appear logical. Giving praise to Him was very important in holy warfare: trumpets, shouting, and singing evoked cataclysmic effects on the enemy.

Though our battles are no longer "against flesh and blood," these Old Testament lessons are true and applicable today.

5

A New Testament View of Spiritual Confrontation

IN LOOKING AT THE NEW TESTAMENT, we find that the lines of battle are more clearly distinguished between spiritual and human. Perhaps in reaction to Jesus' direct self-revelation on earth, the enemy is more clearly and directly the enemy. Because the New Testament Church does not go out and fight military battles, we have no occasion of seeing demonic forces behind military encounters with God's people as we did in the Old Testament. In the New Testament we see demonic forces behind opposition to Jesus and in the events of the Crucifixion and also in opposition to the Church, particularly in the form of persecution.

While a major elucidation of the Old Testament in this context is the identification of demonic spirits with people groups, a major elucidation of the New Testament is the array of spirits. Thus, the Old Testament develops the foundational concept of the large-scale relationship of dark powers to people, and the New Testament continues this by revealing the nature of dark powers, especially through the language used in dealing with them. While in the Old Testament texts we focused on narrative, in the New Testament texts we will focus more on the language and the relation it conveys between the spiritual and the human.

Since the New Testament uses many specific terms related to the powers of darkness, it will be helpful at this point to articulate clear definitions of the various terms, for they are far more than vague generalities.

GREEK TERMS RELATED TO POWERS OF DARKNESS

arche/archai ("principality, first cause")
Plural—Rom. 8:38; Eph. 3:10; 6:12; Col. 1:16; 2:15
Singular—1 Cor. 15:24; Eph. 1:21; Col. 1:16; 2:10

Always signifies primacy, whether in time or rank.[1] Particularly in the plural, it refers to the "organized cosmological powers of angels."[2] Along with the personal term, *archwn,*[3] "principalities" consistently carries the connotation of top-ranking power.

archontwn tou aiwnos toutou ("princes of this age")
1 Cor. 2:6, 8

The *aiwn,* in Gal. 1:4, is identified as being evil. The *archontwn* are *archwn* in the plural, perhaps equivalent to the *archai.* These are apparently high-ranking evil powers under Satan. The phrase itself may also carry a double meaning in reference to the human leaders (Jewish and Roman) who had Jesus crucified, but it is unlikely in this context.

archwn ("prince, ruler")
John 12:31; 14:30; 16:11; Eph. 2:2

The chief authority figure over a given national, organizational, or spiritual realm; used for Satan as above or for human leaders (see Luke 12:58).

daimwn ("demon")

There are many occurrences of this term in the New Testament. It was used by the Greeks to denote gods or lesser deities.[4] In folk belief *daimwn* were spirits of the dead.[5] Only the New Testament clearly distinguishes them as evil (that is, "unclean") spirits. Kittel distinguishes *exousiai* and *archai,* which are "cosmic powers," from *daimones,* "whose region does not extend beyond the *aer"* (the ethereal region above the earth).[6] In agreement with this, the New Testament depicts demons as attaching themselves to or inhabiting humans (even pigs), suggesting that they crave embodiment—whereas the powers of darkness (demonic powers but distinct from demons per se) show no such evidence at all of embodiment, strictly operating from higher positions of domination.

exousia/exousai ("authority, ruling power")

Plural—Eph. 3:10; 6:12; Col. 1:16; 2:15
Singular—1 Cor. 15:24; Eph. 1:21; Col. 2:10

Expresses ability or right to perform an action such that there are no hindrances in the way.[7] In every usage related to the powers of darkness it occurs immediately after *arche -ai,* implying a close connection if not full identification between the two.

dunamis/dunameis ("[supernatural] power, strength")

Rom. 8:38; 1 Cor. 15:24; Eph. 1:21

Expresses the ability to perform an action. Application of the term to angelic beings has its roots in Old Testament usage.[8]

ho archonta tes exousias tou aeros ("the prince of the authority of the air")

Eph. 2:2

> A description of Satan, the archpower, in immediate rule over the "authorities," which are active in the *aer,* the space on or above the earth, where evil spirits were known to dwell.

ho theos tou aiwnos toutou ("the god of this age")

2 Cor. 4:4

> This *aiwn* being evil, the god of it is a generating power of the evil, and in the singular this invariably refers to Satan.

katachthonia ("subterranean, under the earth")

Phil. 2:10

> In Greek usage *"katachthonioi* are always *theoi* or *daimones."*[9] These are strictly spiritual beings and, by New Testament definition, demonic.

kosmokratoras tou skotous toutou ("[world] rulers of this darkness/sin")

Eph. 6:12

> Deeply rooted in astrology, *kosmokratoras* was a term used in Hellenistic mystical writings referring to the seven supreme astrological deities.[10] Here it refers to powerful spirits that Paul says we fight, possibly alluding to astrological deities centered in Ephesus.

kuriotetos/kuriotetes ("angelic dominion or powers")

Eph. 1:21; Col. 1:16

> With roots in the term *kurios,* meaning "lord," it likely refers to a high-ranking classification of angelic powers.

ochurwmatwn ("strongholds")

2 Cor. 10:4

A military term for a "fortified place."[11] Paul uses it to describe the fortification that the powers of darkness have established by way of deception over people's thoughts and attitudes.

pantos onomatos onomazomenou ("every name that can be named"; "every title that can be titled")

Eph. 1:21

A catchall phrase of sorts, expressing Christ's supremacy over every conceivable power, whether or not He has named it. The thrust is that nothing escapes the supremacy of Christ.

pneumatika tes ponerias entois epouraniois ("spiritual evil in the heavenlies")

Eph. 6:12

Probably a "comprehensive designation for all the classes of hostile spirits,"[12] though grammatically (by the use of "and") and contextually (regarding ranks of warring spirits), it may designate a lower-ranking class of dark powers.

stoicheia ("basic or elemental spirits")

Gal. 4:3, 9; Col. 2:8, 20

Originated in Hellenistic astrology, used in reference to star gods.[13] It can also refer to elements of which the world is made or to elemental principles (legalities). The root *stoichos* means "rank" or "row."[14]

theoi polloi kai kurioi polloi ("many gods and many lords")

1 Cor. 8:5

The lesser gods and lords known to the people, identified by Deut. 32:17 and Ps. 106:37 as being demonic. Deut. 10:17 acknowledges the existence of other "gods" and "lords," asserting only that Yahweh is sovereign over them all, which is exactly what Paul acknowledges and asserts here.

thronoi ("thrones")

Col. 1:16

Possibly a reference to one of the highest classes of angels.[15] In this context it may carry the double meaning of human thrones, that is, rulers.

SIGNIFICANT TEXTS RELATED TO POWERS OF DARKNESS

So that analysis of each term may be more clearly and consistently understood both in Paul's usage and in present application, I will again offer my own translation with a slant toward a more literal reading. Wherever appropriate, I will maintain consistency in relating one English term to one Greek term.

Mark 5:9-10—The Gerasene Demoniac

[Jesus] asked him, "What is your name?"

And he replied, "My name is Legion, for we are many." And he begged Him repeatedly not to send them out of the region *(Mark 5:9-10)*.

Here we have what appears to be a predominant demon speaking on behalf of many others. Note how Jesus had absolute authority over these demons. Two questions that almost defy an answer to our human perspective are (1) why did they beg Jesus not to send them out of the region? and (2) why did He cast them into pigs?

Luke 10:17-20—Satan Falls like Lightning

"Lord, even the demons [*daimonia*] submit to us in your name."

And He said to them, "I watched Satan fall like lightning from heaven. Behold, I have given you the authority to tread upon serpents and scorpions, and all the power of the enemy; and nothing by any means will harm you. Nevertheless, do not rejoice that the spirits submit to you, but rejoice that your names have been enrolled in heaven" *(Luke 10:17-20).*

Here we see first of all the direct link between Satan and demons; defeat for one is defeat for the other. There is no compelling reason to identify this as Satan's pre-Adamic fall. It is much more likely an expression of Satan's defeat in the ministry of the 72 who had been sent out. The fall from heaven here is likely something Jesus saw in a vision into the spiritual realm (compare with Rev. 12:7-9).

Second, we see the clear authority that Jesus grants to His followers who act in His name. Serpents were symbolic of demons in Jewish thought. This is not power to survive demonic attacks but to trample over them. Furthermore, we see that in all of this, Jesus' followers will be protected from the evil one's harm. This protection is not tentative, but the term *ou me* is an emphatic negation, signifying "absolutely not" or "no way" will you be harmed.

Finally, Jesus cautions them that their joy is not to be in the victory over the demons. No focus is given to the demonic, neither in fear nor strategizing nor in happily indulging in war stories. Our joy from first to last is to be in the fact that we are saved and known in heaven—that we are God's children.

Acts 13:6-12—Paul's First Missionary Journey

Without quoting the whole story here, we see that Elymas, the sorcerer of Paphos, Cyprus, seems to have had a high degree of control over Sergius Paulus, the political leader of the island. This in turn may have meant he had a high degree of control over the whole island. When Paul bound the power of Elymas and blinded him, his power was obviously broken. Sergius Paulus believed. We cannot know for sure, but this may very likely have had a widespread impact on the island.

1 Cor. 10:19-20—The Eucharist and Idol Feasts

What then do I mean? That meat offered to idols is anything, or that an idol is anything? No, but the things [pagans] sacrifice, they sacrifice to demons *[daimoniois],* not to God *(1 Cor. 10:19-20).*

Paul is saying that neither sacrifices nor the idols to which they are sacrificed have any inherent power, good or evil. But in actuality meat is not sacrificed to the stone image itself but to the spirit represented by or attached to that idol. Thus, pagan sacrifices are, as Deut. 32:17 and Ps. 106:37 assert, done to demons, and Christians are to have no part in it.

Acts of sacrifice are certainly among the primary ways in which demons, and by extension powers of darkness, gain and maintain influence over people.

2 Pet. 2:4—Angels Who Sinned

God did not spare angels when they sinned, but, consigning them to tartarus, delivered them to pits of darkness to be kept for judgment *(2 Pet. 2:4).*

This text, and its parallel in Jude 6, makes an oblique statement on the condition of fallen angels. Most interpretations through history have placed these angels in the same category as the powers of darkness. Indeed, there is little to say that this multitude of spirits has been completely locked up and inactive throughout history. The key question here is what is *tartarus* and how do we interpret "pits of darkness" (Jude says, "in darkness")? In Greek mythology and in Jewish apocalyptic, *tartarus* was thought of as a "subterranean place lower than hades where divine punishment was meted out."[16] In the ancient worldview, heaven (with its various levels), hell, and Hades were all assigned to various places within the known cosmos. The place of evil spirits was subterranean, yet it was acknowledged that they were active in the human sphere. Peter may be taking this term and concept of darkness to refer to the spiritual existence of these fallen angels. Though they run loose through the physical world, spiritually they are in bondage.

THE SPIRITUAL ASPECT OF THE POWERS

These texts, which depict the spiritual nature of the powers, may be subdivided into several categories.

Satan as the Highest Evil Power

Luke 4:5-6—The Devil Tempting Jesus

[The devil] led Him up and showed Him all the king-doms of the [inhabited] earth in a moment of time. And the devil said to Him, "I will give you all their authority and glory, for it has been given to me, and I can give it to whomever I wish" *(Luke 4:5-6)*.

The word *oikoumene* implies the *inhabited* world, not simply the world or the whole world. The devil does not indicate rulership over the uninhabited earth—only where the people are, for it is people, not places, that are deceived. Thus, this text further affirms that his rule is over people and only by extension over the places they inhabit. Note also that Jesus did not deny or revoke this rulership.

John 12:31; 14:30; 16:11—Jesus Nearing the Cross

Now judgment is upon this world; now the prince *[archwn]* of this world will be cast out. . . .

The prince *[archwn]* of this world is coming. . . .

The prince *[archwn]* of this world has now been judged *(John 12:31; 14:30; 16:11)*.

The *archwn* is the chief ruler, the prince of principalities, over a given realm, in this case the world *(kosmos)*. Jesus acknowledges not only Satan's powerful position but also the fact that Satan will be judged and cast out.

Eph. 2:1-2—From Death to Life in Christ

You were dead in your transgressions and sins, in which you used to walk according to the age *[aiwn]* of this world and to the prince of the authority of the air *[archonta tes exousias tou aeros]*, the spirit who is now working in the sons of disobedience *(Eph. 2:1-2)*.

This text perhaps comes closest to identifying the powers of darkness as being behind social forces. The *aiwn* is normally understood as a period of time, consistently identified by Paul as being evil. Evil spirits influence or intensify attitudes and change in a society and define the very nature of the age.

"The prince of the authority of the air" clearly depicts Satan as the highest evil power immediately over the "authorities." The "air" is where the spirits are understood to be active. And Paul knows they have sufficient power to generate evil on a broad social scale.

2 Cor. 4:4—The Gospel Veiled to Unbelievers

The god of this age *[ho theos tou aiwnos toutou]* has blinded the minds of the unbelieving, so that they cannot see the light of the gospel of the glory of Christ, who is the image of God *(2 Cor. 4:4)*.

"This age" is always in contrast to "the age to come," wherein Christ will reign without opposition. Satan, who is "the god of this age," thereby the chief influencer, is described as doing what he has always done best: deceiving.

1 John 5:19—Conclusion of Letter

We know that we are of God and that the whole world *[kosmos]* lies in [the control of] the evil one *[ponerw]* *(1 John 5:19)*.

The term *kosmos* denotes the world as a sphere of humanity, rather than the material world. It lies under the influence of Satan, the embodiment of evil.

THE POWERS OF DARKNESS AS SPIRITS

Rom. 8:38-39—More than Conquerors

I am convinced that neither death nor life, neither angels nor principalities *[archai]*, neither things present *[enestwta]* nor things to come *[mellonta]*, nor powers *[dunameis]*, nor height *[hupswma]*, nor depth *[bathos]*, nor anything else in all creation will be able to separate us from the love of God that is in Christ Jesus our Lord *(Rom. 8:38-39)*.

Paul reminds us that the powers of darkness have no ability to separate us from God. Lee finds intriguing astrological backgrounds to some of these terms: "Here, 'height' *(hupswma)* and 'depth' *(bathos)* are technical terms of astrology, denoting the highest and lowest points reached by a heavenly body. . . . 'Things present' *(enestwta)* and 'things to come' *(mellonta)* also refer to the present a future position of a star."[17] Even these common words had whole arenas of cosmic usage to the contemporary readers. Paul is assuring the Church that as much as powers of darkness affect people's lives, God will not allow them or any situation to separate us from Him.

1 Cor. 2:6-8—Wisdom from the Spirit

We do speak wisdom among the mature, wisdom not of this age or of the princes of this age *[archontwn tou aiwnos toutou]*, who are coming to nothing; but we speak of God's wisdom in a mystery. . . . None of the princes of this age *[archontwn tou aiwnos toutou]* had understood it, for if they understood it, they would not have crucified the Lord of glory *(1 Cor. 2:6-8)*.

This text corresponds to the terms and concepts of Gal. 1:4. Some understand it as referring to human rulers (that is, the Jews or the Romans). Yet Paul's choice of words is clearly that of the powers of darkness. His phrase "are coming to nothing" makes some sense when applied to human rulers, but when applied to spiritual powers, it is fully consistent with Jesus', Pauline, and Johannine thought. These evil powers are coming to nothing in that they meet defeat at the Cross, defeat at the hands of the Church, and ultimate defeat on the Day of Judgment. Note again the implication that the powers of darkness are working through humans to do their intent.

1 Cor. 8:5—Food Sacrificed to Idols

Even if there are so called gods, whether in heaven or on earth, as indeed there are many "gods" and many "lords" *[theoi polloi kai kurioi polloi]*, yet for us there is but one God *(1 Cor. 8:5)*.

These gods and lords command power over those who offer sacrifices to them. This is never disputed. But Yahweh is above them all. The *katachthonia* ("[beings] under the earth") of Phil. 2:10 would be included here.

2 Cor. 10:3-5—Overthrowing Strongholds

Though we walk in the flesh, we do not wage war according to the flesh. The weapons of our warfare are not of the flesh, but are powerful in God to overthrow *[kathairesin]* strongholds *[ochurwmatwn]*, overthrowing false reasoning and every proud obstacle raised up against the knowledge of God, and we are taking every thought captive to the obedience of Christ *(2 Cor. 10:3-5)*.

Paul unequivocally states that our war is not physical or human. It can therefore only be spiritual. Our spiritual weapons are so powerful that we are actually able to wreak destruction on strongholds ("fortified places" of evil). The verb *kathairew* can mean to "pull down," "destroy," or "overthrow." This is what God intends for us to do in holy warfare. Strongholds, as Paul sees them, have to do with the human mind. That is, powers of darkness establish entrenched deceptions in peoples' beliefs, thinking, feelings, attitudes, will, even entire paradigms of their worldview. Just like our weapons, the strongholds are not physical or human. Their functional nature is to deceive people away from a saving knowledge of God. And, as Paul implies, when strongholds are overthrown, people's minds will come under obedience to Christ.

THE SPIRITUAL BATTLE FROM THE CROSS TO THE SECOND COMING

Col. 2:15—Alive in Christ

Having stripped off the principalities *[archas]* and authorities *[exousias]*, He made a public spectacle of them, triumphing over them in it [the Cross] *(Col. 2:15)*.

"Stripped off" is in the Greek middle voice, which here is primarily concerned with that which interests the self, meaning that God in Christ stripped off the powers for His own victory. Most commentators take this position, and Heb. 2:14 supports this as well. We can only surmise that the demonic powers delighted in Christ's suffering and death, without knowing that what they thought was their victory was actually part of God's redemptive plan all along.

Though in appearance a defeat, Christ's sacrifice on the Cross, making atonement for all people, was a victory upsetting the principalities and authorities. The public spectacle may refer to those who witnessed the Crucifixion and later understood its meaning. It may also refer to angelic and demonic beings in the spiritual realm, for only they could fully see this triumph over the principalities and authorities. Our present-day victory over the powers of darkness, then, is rooted in Christ's redemptive work on the Cross, and all those powers know it.

Eph. 3:10—Paul, the Preacher to the Gentiles

So that now, through the Church, the manifold wisdom of God should be made known to the principalities and authorities in the heavenly realms *[archais kai tais exousiais en tois epouraniois] (Eph. 3:10).*

The Church is actually God's channel to make himself known to the principalities and authorities. This verse implies that, rather than taking a passive or a teaching role toward the powers, the Church has confrontational contact with the powers of darkness. That God intends for the Church to confront these powers is important, because "the Church alone is Christ's body and fullness [and] only through the Church can the principalities and authorities be shown with clarity the claim of Christ's lordship."[18] It also verifies where those powers are—not within organizations or social phenomena, but in the heavenly realms.

Eph. 6:12—Spiritual Warfare

Our struggle is not against flesh and blood, but against the principalities *[archas],* against the authorities *[exousias],* against the rulers of this darkness *[kosmokratoras tou skotous toutou]* and against the spiritual forces of evil in the heavenly realms *[pneumatika tes ponerias entois epouraniois] (Eph. 6:12).*

This verse is the climax of Paul's exhortations to the Church on this cosmic war. No text is clearer that the focus of our fight is against spiritual powers, not earthly. Lincoln notes that the term *pale* (battle) usually denotes a wrestling match.[19] It is not a distant battle, but one up close in which we must grapple. The titles *archas* and *exousias* can be traced to possible connections with Artemis and to Isis or Sarapis; then to other lesser astrological deities, the *kosmokratoras;* then the more general category of evil spirits, or perhaps lower-ranking spirits, the *pneumatika.* Paul's general implication is that when the battle is won in the heavenly realms, it is won on earth.

1 Cor. 15:24-26—The Resurrection of the Dead

Then the end will come, when He hands over the kingdom to the God and Father, when He has destroyed all principality *[archen]*, authority *[exousian]* and power *[dunamin]*. For He must reign until He has put all His enemies under His feet. The last enemy to be destroyed is death *(1 Cor. 15:24-26)*.

Paul's terms here are intended as being inclusive because the very last enemy, death, will be destroyed. Despite the presence of the powers of darkness, Paul still asserts that Christ is reigning and will continue to reign to the end. These verses could be construed as both of the spiritual and the human realm, but the apocalyptic context presses for a spiritual interpretation.

THE HUMAN ASPECT OF THE POWERS

Rom. 13:1-2—Submission to Authorities

Everyone must submit himself to the governing authorities *[exousiais]*, for there is no authority *[exousia]* except that which God has established. The authority *[exousia]* that exists has been established by God. Consequently, he who rebels against the authority *[exousia]* is rebelling against what God has instituted, and those who do so will bring judgment on themselves *(Rom. 13:1-2)*.

Titus 3:1—Paul's Charge to Titus

Remind them to be subject to principalities *[archais]*, to authorities *[exousiais]*, to be obedient, to be ready for every good work *(Titus 3:1)*.

The nature and operation of human versus spiritual powers has been debated more in Rom. 13 than in any other text. Though these two texts overtly refer to the earthly state, even here there is more than meets the eye. Oscar Cullmann comments on this chapter:

Romans 13 does not belong in a secular Greek context, but in a Jewish-hellenistic context, and indeed a theological, or more precisely, a Pauline one. In this context the word *exousiai* definitely has a two-fold meaning. Not only was the meaning "angelic powers" current to the early Christian reader, but we may say even more. For Paul, in any case, the plural *exousiai* and the plurally used singular *pasa exousia* mean in every other instance *only* "invisible powers."[20]

G. H. C. MacGregor goes even further to ask, is Paul "again hinting that State authority is to be thought of merely as the executive agent of angelic or demonic powers?"[21] This may be going too far, but we can say that when the state is referenced in the New Testament, it seems to carry the implicit understanding that spiritual influences play a role in the state's activities, whether overt or behind the scenes.

The Stoicheia

Gal. 4:3, 9—Becoming Children of God

So also we, while we were children, were enslaved under the elemental spirits [basic principles] of the world *[stoicheia tou kosmou]*. . . . But now that you know God, or rather are known by God, how is it that you turn back to those weak and worthless elemental spirits [basic principles—*stoicheia*] to which you wish to be enslaved all over again? *(Gal. 4:3, 9)*.

Col. 2:8, 20—Dead, Alive in Christ

See to it that no one takes you captive through philosophy and empty deception, according to human tradition, according to the elemental spirits [basic principles] of the world *[stoicheia tou kosmou]*, and not according to Christ. . . . If you died with Christ from the elemental spirits [basic principles] of the world *[stoicheiwn tou kosmou]*, why, as if you were still living in the world, do you submit to its rules? *(Col. 2:8, 20).*

The contrasting contexts of these two churches (Judaizers in Galatia and false pagan teaching in Colosse) combined with the consistency of Paul's language in both would encourage a broad understanding of the *stoicheia* rather than one specific interpretation. On one hand, *stoicheia* refers to basic fundamentals of language, ideas, or the physical elements (2 Pet. 3:10, 12); on the other hand *stoicheia* refers to heavenly bodies and spirits. We are very likely facing the same type of situation as in Rom. 13:1-2 and Titus 3:1, where we see that spiritual powers operate behind the guise of earthly elements. Lee adds, "Every element was thought to have its god, so that the word *stoicheia* came to be used of these elemental deities and spirits."[22] Thus, to speak of material things is to simultaneously speak of the *stoicheia* as spirits. The influence of these lower-ranking gods of astrology had brought the people to the point of slavish bondage.

THE SUPREMACY OF CHRIST OVER THE POWERS

Eph. 1:21—Exaltation of Christ

Far above all principality *[arches]* and authority *[exousias]* and power *[dunamews]* and [angelic] dominion *[kuriotetos]*, and every name that can be named *[pantos onomatos onomazomenou]*, not only in this age, but also in the one to come *(Eph. 1:21).*

Col. 1:16—The Supremacy of Christ

By him were created all things in heaven and on earth, visible and invisible, whether thrones *[thronoi]* or [angelic] dominions *[kuriotetes]* or principalities *[archai]* or authorities *[exousiai]*; all things have been created through him and for him *(Col. 1:16).*

Col. 2:9-10—Fullness in Christ

In Him all the fullness of the Deity lives in bodily form, and you have been given fullness in Him who is the Head over every principality [arches] and authority [exousias] (Col. 2:9-10).

These three preceding texts express Christ's position of absolute power over the array of powers. They are not necessarily listed in descending order (contrast Eph. 1:21 with Col. 1:16). It may be argued that Col. 1:16 and 2:9-10 refer to God's angelic hierarchy—and this may well be so. A distinction between good and evil is not made. The point is that Christ is supreme over all created powers, good or evil. Furthermore, at the time of their creation, the hierarchy of angelic powers was entirely good; an evil hierarchy took shape only after the Fall. So the point of these verses remains applicable: Christ is still sovereign over them all.

While Eph. 1:21 clarifies that Christ's supremacy extends through this age and the age to come, Col. 1:16 clarifies that this supremacy covers both spiritual powers in heaven and human powers on earth. This passage gives the clearest representation of the dual spiritual and human nature of the powers.

APOCALYPTIC INSIGHTS

Rev. 2:13—To the Church in Pergamum

I know where you live, where the throne of Satan is, and you hold fast to My name. You did not deny My faith even in the days of Antipas, My faithful witness, who was put to death among you, where Satan lives (Rev. 2:13).

In Pergamum was an enormous statue of Zeus, the supreme god of the Greek pantheon. This enthronement stood in direct confrontation to God. John's statement may mean that Satan has used this great altar as a direct point of contact between the spiritual and natural world to gain a hold over the people. A second, equally significant problem as part of the Roman Empire was that Pergamum was "the official cult center of emperor worship in Asia."[23] Because of that, Mounce states, "It was here that Satan had established his official seat or chair of state. As Rome had become the center of Satan's activity in the West . . . so Pergamum had become his "throne" in the East. . . . Little wonder that martyrdom begins in Pergamum."[24] Countless implications can be drawn from this in relation to present-day idolatry and other forms of compliance with the demonic, as well as to demonically inspired political or social forces.

Rev. 13:1, 7, 11-12—The Beasts Out of the Sea and the Land

> I saw a beast coming up out of the sea. . . . And it was given to him to make war with the saints and to overcome them. And he was given authority over every tribe, people, language, and nation. . . . And I saw another beast, coming up out of the earth. . . . He exercised all the authority of the first beast before him, and makes the earth and its inhabitants worship the first beast *(Rev. 13:1, 7, 11-12)*.

The rising of these "beasts," however they are to be interpreted, is in a way a culmination of the dominance of spirits to the point of every people group being under the grip of Satan himself.

SUMMARY OF NEW TESTAMENT TEXTS

The many specific terms used to describe the powers of darkness seem to affirm that they are not to be thought of as some nebulous force of evil but as personified beings, each having some kind of distinction and ranking within the whole panoply of evil. Some of the same terms and concepts used in the Old Testament are used in the New—for example, "princes." Technical terms show that we are dealing with spirits that have distinct identities and rank. But the New Testament does not concern itself with their identity or rank, only with the superior power of Jesus Christ, who triumphs over them all.

Satan's work is brought down by believers who operate under the authority of Christ. Satan's judgment and defeat are linked to the Cross. Yet Satan is still depicted as being alive and at work in unbelievers while at enmity toward the Church. At the end of time Satan and all the powers of darkness will be totally destroyed.

The Church is God's temporal instrument for confronting the powers of evil, and this confrontation is more spiritual than physical. Yet the spiritual powers operate through human beings, their ideas and institutions.

Jesus does not address beliefs related to pagan gods (for example, when the woman at the well in John 4:20 implies the pervasive assumption that worship of gods was to be done relative to geographical areas). Jesus, rather, reaffirms the Old Testament proclamation that the one true God is universal and is not geographically bound, a position in harmony with all New Testament texts.

Where Jesus' Lordship is affirmed, the powers of darkness are frequently mentioned as being under submission to Him. This is important to remember not just for doctrinal clarity but for affirming our victory over these powers of darkness. When the Lordship of Christ is manifest in the Church, the powers of darkness are disarmed, and the masses of humanity are freed from their dominion. Jesus' Lordship is absolute, and believers are privileged to call upon His authority.

Focus in holy warfare should be as it is in Scripture—not on the demonic, but on Christ. And our joy is not to be in overcoming the powers of darkness, but in our relationship with God.

6

A Theological Assessment

IN THE BIBLE, holy warfare is never seen as an end in itself. It is a means of spreading the gospel. What it is we are warring against is sometimes debated, so how we are to respond largely depends on our understanding of these opposing forces.

THEOLOGICAL ASSESSMENTS OF POWERS OF DARKNESS

While German writers had previously been discussing the nature of dark powers in relation to Nazi Germany, the 1950s and early 1960s saw the linking of these powers to attitudes or propensities of sociopolitical structures and social forces—in a word, demythologization. Among them the actual existence of spiritual beings is held in suspicion. Thus, they interpret earthly systems and structures as being the real manifestation of the so-called cosmic powers.[1] Walter Wink, a leading contemporary figure of this general view, essentially restates their case, attempting to strengthen its exegetical and historical foundation.[2] Social activists have a similar problem of having to equate the powers with earthly systems. One example here is John Yoder, who also arrives at similar conclusions.[3]

All of these positions reflect a worldview that is in varying degrees closed to the supernatural and does not recognize the "middle zone," so that the meaning of the biblical text invariably becomes truncated. Furthermore, if the powers are manifestations of structures, why do some structures turn evil while others do not?

O'Brien discusses problems with the view of dark powers as structures: "First, we do not have an adequate explanation as to why structures do not always become tyrannical. Second, we unjustifiably restrict our understanding of the malevolent activity of Satan, whereas he is too versatile to be limited to the structural. . . . Third, we become too negative toward society and its structures. . . . Some structures may be changed for good."[4] Social or political systems are not the primary place to be looking for cosmic powers. We have little biblical evidence to affirm this. Systems are human constructs, whether philosophical, religious, political, economic, social, technological, or military. They can be used for good or evil. The real question is—Who influences them?

However spirits may have gained influence in each individual case, we can see now that across the earth they have blinded people's eyes to the gospel message. How people are blinded varies. The degree to which spirits initiate thoughts and behavior versus manipulate what the people themselves initiate is debatable. But ample evidence suggests that the two sides—human carnality and the demonic—are inextricably interrelated.

THE NATURE OF THE POWERS

While the Old Testament is replete with tales of war, the New Testament continues the war imagery in the spiritual sphere. Military terms can be found throughout the New Testament. Faith is "the good fight." Protection is by "the armor of God." The Word of God is "a sword." Satan's attacks are "fiery darts." The Christian is a "soldier of Christ Jesus." And Jesus himself is seen as being in continual war with evil powers, even appearing in Rev. 19:11-16 as a warrior on a white horse. 1 John 3:8 states succinctly, "The reason the Son of God appeared was to destroy the devil's work." And when stating that "the gates of Hades will not overcome" or "stand against" the forward movement of the Church, Jesus clarifies both that the Church is central to this war and that the Church will win. Much of the Early Church's history, particularly whenever it moved forward, included holy warfare, though it was not necessarily given a name.

In looking at biblical texts, we should ask what these powers are against which we stand. How human are they? How spiritual are they? The Greek terms *arche, exousia, dynamis,* and *thronos* are commonly used for spiritual beings, but they also refer to earthly governments and political power—for example, Rom. 13:1; 1 Cor. 2:6; Titus 3:1; and 1 Pet. 2:13. Some argue that when these terms are used, they refer to earthly political or socioeconomic powers and the evil they might inspire. But texts such as Eph. 3:10 and Col. 2:15 can hardly be interpreted in any way but spiritual. Still other uses of these terms and others in 1 Cor. 15:24; Eph. 1:21 *(kyriotes);* Col. 1:16 and 2:10 can be interpreted both as earthly and as heavenly realities. Yet the meanings of the words themselves are rooted in astrology and the names of deities.

Cullmann has done the foremost work in deciphering Paul's fluid usage of the same terms for dark powers as well as governments (see Rom. 13:1-5) as being dual in meaning. He says, "The actual State authority is thought of as the executive agent of angelic powers," and conversely, "the invisible angelic powers stand behind the State government."[5] This is to say that Paul uses the terms fluidly, and given all sides, the terms can now mean earthly powers, then spiritual—or both. This deliberately fluid use of terms is important in discerning case by case how holy warfare is to be engaged. Thus, while remembering that we "wrestle not against flesh and blood," we know that the spiritual is always behind flesh and blood. Our focus must be dual and attentive to both.

We cannot say that all humans are under literal control of either God or of demons, for Scripture speaks much of the fleshly, or carnal, nature of people who act willfully (for example, Gal. 5:19-21). But Luke 4:5-7 and 1 John 5:19 indicate that human societies and systems are under some degree of Satan's influence. Thus, while holy warfare prioritizes prayer, it involves more than prayer. It involves all of earthly life: social, political, economic, and ethical—both in personal and in public realms.

SPIRITUAL HIERARCHIES

Etymology and usage of biblical terms indicate that some demonic figures are superior and of a different character than others. At the top is Satan; below him are principalities and authorities, thrones, world rulers, dominions, powers, demons, and elemental spirits. The fluid use of these terms in Scripture suggests that it is not important for us to know the ranks of these dark powers.

Paul did name the powers in Ephesians and elsewhere, and Jesus ascertained a demon's name (Luke 8:30). They sought to specifically identify what they were dealing with, though they did not get lost in any kind of demonology. In either of these cases, we can say that there are no explicit biblical teachings for or against ascertaining the names of spirits. The scriptural objective when dealing with any form of the demonic is to do the work of God and to expand His kingdom.

Dan. 10:21 and 12:1 indicate that the angel Michael is a "prince," and the distinction between cherubim and seraphim together imply some kind of hierarchy among the angels of

God. But again Scripture does not make it any of our business to understand their ranks, but rather to do the work of God.

HOW DOES HUMAN SIN RELATE TO DEMONIC SPIRITS?

How do humans and their activities influence the powers of darkness? A look at biblical texts finds, for example, that worship at the high places and spreading trees (Deut. 12:2) are characteristic locations for the invocations of "gods," the same term used for the dark powers. Worship employing sacred stones and Asherah poles (Exod. 34:13-14) also indicates Asherah as a major "god" or demonic spirit. Worship of Baals and the Ashtoreths (Judg. 2:11-15) unites the people with other "gods." Meat sacrificed to idols (1 Cor. 10:18-22) is communing with demons in the way that Christians commune with Christ in the Eucharist. In the context of anger, Eph. 4:26-27 indicates that sin gives the devil a foothold. Regarding forgiveness, 2 Cor. 2:11 says, "We are not unaware of his schemes." The widespread embracing of sin also seems to give demonic powers a stronghold and begets the wrath of God among foreign nations as well as Israel and Judah before their exiles. The apocalyptic prophecies of the New Testament (for example, Matt. 24, 2 Thess. 2, Rev. 13) indicate the wickedness that will overcome much of the human race and lead to the final domination of evil powers. Human carnality and the supernatural forces of evil go hand in hand.

GOD AND SATAN'S POWERS

If our sovereign, omnipotent God has given humanity the freedom to rebel and turn against Him, is this not also the case with spiritual beings, as Scripture repeatedly depicts? Unlike people, who are redeemable, Scripture gives no indication that spirits will be redeemed. Rather, evil powers in rebellion against God will meet only eternal torment (see Matt. 8:29; Luke 8:31; 1 Cor. 15:24; Rev. 20:10).

Neither Jesus nor Paul nor other apostles or prophets ever challenged the fact that the kingdoms of this world are under the influence of Satan. Wesley also affirmed this, saying of evil angels, "They are (remember, so far as God permits!) *kosmo-kratores,*—governors of the world!"[6] But Scripture is equally clear that far from being equal to God's power, Satan's power is limited, and he acts only within the bounds God has set.

Scripture never says God wiped out or annihilated the powers of darkness. It does say that Satan is a defeated enemy whom God will "crush" under our feet (Rom. 16:20), that his doom is sure (Rev. 20), that the saints will suffer (2 Tim. 3:12) but will overcome "by the blood of the Lamb and by the word of their testimony" (Rev. 12:11). Satan knows this and so acts in a wounded desperation, "filled with fury, because he knows that his time is short" (v. 12). The analogy of D-day is sometimes used here. On June 6, 1944, the Allied forces launched an all-out offensive on the Axis forces when they invaded Normandy. The heavy loss broke the back of Nazi Germany, and from that point on the Nazis were a defeated enemy—*but they still fought on.* Michael Green expresses it this way:

> There was no denying that the critical battle had been won. The Axis forces could look forward to nothing but final defeat. But the war went on. They refused to accept defeat until they had to. Sometimes considerable success attended their struggle. Often the appearances looked favourable for them. But nothing could alter the fact that they were doomed. The ultimate Victory Day would dawn, as it did in 1945. That is how it is with Satan.[7]

Though Jesus overcame Satan's temptations in the desert and triumphed over him on the Cross, Satan still fights on like a rabid dog—doomed but dangerous until the end.

OUR AUTHORITY IN CHRIST

Jesus said, "All authority in heaven and on earth has been given to me" (Matt. 28:18). We go as His representatives, exercising His authority, for He said, "I will do whatever you ask in my name" (John 14:13). Gal. 2:20 makes clear that "Christ lives in me." In fact, the New Testament is replete with affirmations of our identity in Christ: we are chosen, children of God, temples of His Spirit, heirs, saints, justified, righteous, holy, citizens of heaven, seated in the heavenly realms.

The problem is that many believers do not exercise their God-given authority in Christ. Even those who have experienced sanctification may not necessarily go beyond their experience to grasp the full extent of their new identity in Christ by exercising its authority. When people don't feel it, they usually give it cognitive recognition but do not live it. Believers are given authority to resist dark powers and to appeal before the very throne of God. The question is—Do we exercise that authority?

A policeman has the same legal authority whether he has 1 or 20 years of experience. But the more experienced one will know more of how to exercise his authority and of what he can and cannot do. So also Christians are given authority in Christ, but just as there is salvation, sanctification, and growth in maturity, so also young or unaware believers will not exercise that authority the way a battle-worn believer will.

Jesus gave His disciples authority to drive evil spirits out of people and to heal them (Matt. 10:1). But we have no evidence that this authority extends to driving demons out of neighborhoods, cities, or any other place. There is a reason for this: every neighborhood, city, or other location will have people who live in ways that open doors for Satan to come in and rule. Thus, we can no more cast some spirit out of a place of pagan worship or out of a city than we can drive demons out of people who do things to welcome them. For, as Jesus says, the evil spirit will go out and get seven others even more wicked than itself to go back into the person (Luke 11:24-26). To presume we can do this defies God's whole order of sin and its consequences as well as the order of free will and its results. We are never told or given an example to attempt to pull down high-ranking powers of darkness from cities or organizations. Scripture does not tell us to ask God to *make* people Christian or to expel demonic opposition.

What we ask God for is His grace to bind the powers of darkness and open the minds of unbelievers. We plead God's mercy and prevenient grace upon people lost in sin, who, as with all of us, do not deserve anything from God, so that they may have greater freedom from demonic deception to make a decision for Christ. This is where evangelism enters—and finds greater effectiveness when people have prayed.

One thing must be clear: We do not have authority over people's minds or their fleshly inclination to sin. Jesus never gave us authority over sinners. What we have authority over is the spiritual world that influences them. People's own hardness of heart may cause the struggle for their salvation and spiritual freedom to go on for years. Our authority in the spiritual realm is so that they may have greater freedom to make that decision for Christ.

THE ISSUE OF STRONGHOLDS

The issue of strongholds is central to the discussion of the effects of dark powers, for it is precisely in strongholds where we encounter them. Tom White succinctly describes a stronghold as "an entrenched pattern of thought, an ideology, value or behavior that is contrary to the word and will of God."[8] The term occurs in 2 Cor. 10:3-5:

> Though we walk in the flesh, we do not wage war according to the flesh. The weapons of our warfare are not of the flesh, but are powerful in God to overthrow strong-

holds, overthrowing false reasoning and every proud obstacle raised up against the knowledge of God, and we are taking every thought captive to the obedience of Christ *(author's translation)*.

"Stronghold" *[ochurwma]* is a military term meaning "fortified place." It occurs frequently in the Old Testament in reference to physical fortresses, and the Septuagint uses the term to refer to God as our stronghold. Use of the term in relation to powers of darkness is essentially limited to 2 Cor. 10:4.

Paul elaborates on strongholds by using two terms. One is *logismos* (translated as "thought," "reasoning," or "argument"). It has to do with the intellect, with what people think, and it has been humanity's downfall ever since Eve and Adam hungered after the tree of the knowledge of good and evil. The other term is *hupsoma* (translated as "height," "proud obstacle," or "pretension"). This may relate to human arrogance, though according to the *New International Dictionary of New Testament Theology,* it "probably reflects astrological ideas . . . and hence denotes cosmic powers. Rom. 8:39 and 2 Cor. 10:5 are both concerned with powers directed against God, seeking to intervene between God and man."[9] Either way one interprets it, the demonic intertwines with the flesh.

Strongholds then may be understood as existing on different levels. The most basic is personal: a spirit may have a stronghold over an individual: the Gerasene demoniac, Judas and Elymas, for example. Individual strongholds may be religious, psychological, emotional, intellectual, or sin-related. They are limited to that person and his or her immediate domain of activity. Another level is corporate: there were certainly strongholds among Israel's hostile neighbors; there may have been a stronghold among the Sanhedrin in Jesus' time; Paul encountered strongholds among hostile groups. Corporate strongholds may be religious, occultic, political, social, economic, or sin-related, and they often have long histories.

Paul says we are to "overthrow" them. The verb *kathairew* can also mean to "pull down," "tear down," "destroy," or "overthrow." This does not mean to fret, theologize, or ignore. We are clearly called to action. Since strongholds are described in terms of arrogance and deceit, they are best overthrown with truth. The truth of God's Word, as it is written and as it is lived out in us, will overthrow these proud obstacles regardless of human or demonic origin.

GRACE

Where does grace fit in? Everywhere, in fact. Our authority in Christ is by grace. No matter what we do, were it not for grace, we would have no authority. The kind of authority we have in Jesus' name is greater than anything we can earn or gain by any amount of merit. The very fact that we are allowed to call on His name is by the grace of God. What we say or do in His name is fundamentally relational. We act in His name because we are His children, and that relationship is by grace.

It is grace that opens the minds of unbelievers. How else but by God's going before us, whether or not in answer to prayer, could anyone be saved in a world that is described as being under the control of the evil one? In the act of binding the powers of darkness, God manifests grace toward those under demonic deception and lost in sin so that they may make a move toward Christ.

God thus invites us to participate with Him in the task of building His kingdom, and as we pray, we plead God's grace for unbelievers, that demonic powers would be bound and believers freed to make a decision regarding Christ. We essentially ask that God's grace would cause fruit to be born through us.

THE POWER OF HOLINESS

The power of holiness is the power of the Holy Spirit. The power of the Spirit gives us victory over sin. True victory over sin does not consist of legalistically avoiding forms of evil, but in pursuing righteousness, which has no place for evil. New desires expel the old. This is not a dour holiness, but a holiness of joy that delights in the Lord and finds sin a hindrance and a curse. Victory over sin is essential to anyone who resists the devil, for it is often through sin that the devil weakens and ruins those who would oppose him.

The power of holiness means Spirit-filled living. We cannot live this life by human effort, and at its very best, human effort will fall short. This life is not lived by a formula to be followed, but by a relationship to be entered. In this living relationship, we "keep in step with the Spirit" (Gal. 5:25), who pours into us "all the fullness of God" (Eph. 3:19). The Holy Spirit convicts us of both sin and righteousness (John 16:8). In the Spirit-filled life, we must align ourselves with God in how we think and in how we act. Holy warfare without Spirit-filled living is actually a dangerous proposition. We need the purity of heart that comes from a close walk with God to be victorious in this battle.

The power of holiness means Spirit-empowered ministry, in which the life of holiness that we ourselves live is shared with and transferred to other people. These people are often lost and in bondage to sin and the devil. But Jesus states in Acts 1:8 that power is given to us when the Holy Spirit comes upon us. The baptism of the Holy Spirit both cleanses and empowers. It is a power to witness with a godly courage. It is power to heal and power to resist evil and temptation. We do not fear dark powers but exercise our authority in Christ by the power of His Spirit, expressing His truth that outshines all dark deception.

PRAYER

Prayer is our privilege of speaking directly with God. It is His grace and His authority that make everything happen. In Scripture prayer is consistently motivated by love for God's people and His kingdom. We especially see this in Paul's relationship with

His churches. He prayed for his people because he loved them. And that love was engendered by his love for the Lord.

Though God can act however He wills, He has obviously chosen to act in coordination with our prayers. Jesus tells us to pray that the Lord of the harvest would send out workers, pray persistently like the widow, pray boldly like the friend at midnight, and ask if we want anything to be given. He insists that through prayer we participate in His divine activity.

Prayer is directed to God, not necessarily against demons. In Scripture we observe Jesus, the disciples, Peter, and Paul rebuking demonic spirits. But rebuking a demon should not be confused or mixed with prayer; we have no biblical example or mandate for praying to God and in the next breath rebuking the devil, then shifting back to prayer. Prayer is to our sovereign, loving Heavenly Father.

Nowhere does Scripture give us authority to make boisterous claims against the devil or any high-ranking demonic spirit. While ministering in Japan, I saw two extremes of this. The more common was those who made claims of pulling down demons from over cities, with no forthcoming evidence of anything having happened. The more dangerous was that of a young man who over a period of several months "cast out" the spirits of shrines whenever he passed them on the street. By the end of that period he literally went mad. He was physically loaded on board a plane in a straitjacket and sent back to the United States. Jude 9 tells us that even the archangel Michael, for all his authority (see Dan. 10—12), "did not dare to bring a slanderous accusation against him [the devil], but said, 'the Lord rebuke you!'" It is the Lord's name and authority under which we operate.

A LIFE OF LOVE

Demonic opposition always seems to connect in some way to human relationships. This should come as no surprise, since demonic influence is through people. In every one of his churches, Paul had serious problems. People were divided over false doctrines, spiritual gifts, moral downfalls, and differences in their philosophical and religious backgrounds. Church conflicts are much the same today. Paul faced church problems head on but with a dual understanding of the battle. On one hand he acknowledged the influence of evil spirits; on the other hand he called people to accountability. Spirits or no spirits, believers were to turn from sinfulness and act as followers of Christ.

This is a primary way in which a life of love becomes a major part of overcoming the powers of darkness. Col. 3:12-14 describes virtues expected of God's people: compassion, kindness, humility, gentleness, patience, forbearance, and forgiveness. Then over all of them we are to "put on love, which binds them all together in perfect unity." When people conflict, they tend to see the other party as the problem. But Paul affirms that "our struggle is not against flesh and blood, but against . . . the powers of this dark world and against the spiritual forces of evil in the heavenly realms" (Eph. 6:12). Maintaining humility and love toward all whom we know deprives dark powers of the foothold they need to sabotage relationships within the Church.

Our evangelism is no better than the Christian witness of how we live our lives. How we live either confirms or denies what we profess. On the grassroots level a lifestyle of love is really our greatest means of evangelism. When Jesus said that all people will know we are His disciples if we love one another (John 13:35), He affirmed that love is essential to the very nature of evangelism. Love toward nonbelievers opens hearts and short-circuits openings for demonic deception so that people's eyes are more freely opened and they more readily choose to follow the Lord.

THE MESSAGE OF HOPE

The strong message of hope coming through Scripture is that while the present world order has been under the influence of powerful spirits, in Christ we are not only freed from those influences, but we have authority over them. And through all that we will face in this spiritual war, we will say, "Thanks be to God! He gives us the victory through our Lord Jesus Christ" (1 Cor. 15:57).

7

A Biblical and Practical Response

FROM FIRST TO LAST, Scripture states, implies, demonstrates, and repeats that the battle is the Lord's (for example, 2 Chron. 20:15). Moses tells Israel that the Lord will fight for them and they need only be still (Exod. 14:14). Moses' confrontations with Pharaoh, the resulting plagues, and Israel's deliverance rest squarely on the power of God. In every one of Israel's battles, it was the Lord who brought the victory or allowed defeat. The Lord sent the Midianites fleeing from Gideon (Judg. 7), the Arameans from Samaria (2 Kings 7:3-20), and the Philistines from Jonathan (1 Sam. 14:12-23). He went ahead of (or over) David in the tops of the balsam trees to strike down the Philistines (2 Sam. 5:22-25). Each time David went into battle, he inquired of the Lord and obeyed. Thus, "The LORD gave David victory wherever he went" (2 Sam. 8:14). The Lord gave Elijah success in his power encounter on Mount Carmel (1 Kings 18:16-39) and blinded the Aramean army at Elisha's word (2 Kings 6:13-19).

Is there a key ingredient in all this? Hiebert finds that "the central issue in biblical warfare is not power. For example, in the Old Testament, both the victories and defeats of Israel are attributed to God. Their victory is due to their faithfulness to God and His laws; their defeat is God's punishment for their forsaking Him."[1] The Lord's promise that five would chase a hundred and a hundred chase ten thousand (Lev. 26:8) is based entirely on obedience. Those who disobeyed—such as Achan, Saul, numerous kings of the divided kingdom, and repeatedly Israel as a whole—incurred the Lord's punishment. Those who obeyed experienced His victory.

Likewise, in the New Testament Jesus is in full authority over every demon, and Satan is unable to overcome Him through temptation. Through the Cross, Jesus triumphs over the cosmic powers (John 12:31; Col. 2:15), and He presently reigns over them (Eph. 1:21; Phil. 2:10-11; Col. 1:16; 2:9-10). Since the battle is the Lord's, the promise to His Church is that the gates of Hades will not prevail against it (Matt. 16:18).

Next let us survey several narratives in the Old Testament and several in the New that cover representative texts from which we may draw principles.

OLD TESTAMENT PRECEDENTS

Gen. 12:6-7: At Abram's first sighting of the Promised Land, he faced the problem of the Canaanites' living there. Not just any old tree, but a famous tree, "the great tree of Moreh," stood there. In almost any animistic culture, as the Canaanites were, great or unusual natural formations or trees are often said to be the abode of spirits. With his animistic background in Ur, Abram would likely have been aware of this. His building of an altar to worship at the site of that tree was a deliberate act of praise in the presence of God and in the face of whatever may have opposed him, human or otherwise. He immediately repeated the process at Bethel in verses 8-9. Much later, in Gen.

35:4, Jacob buried pagan artifacts under that same significant tree, immediately after which they experienced extraordinary powers of God.

Exod. 17:8-13: When Israel battled the Amalekites, some did the physical work, and others, here the one with the highest spiritual authority, interceded along with a supporting team. Moses held the staff he performed miracles with (4:17), a symbol of authority. The raising of hands has throughout Scripture been associated with prayer, as well as praise (for example, 1 Kings 8:22-54; Ezra 9:5; Pss. 28:2; 77:2; 134:2; 143:6; 1 Tim. 2:8). The connection between Moses' raising of his hands and the Israelites winning, then lowering his hands and the Israelites losing, marks the human effect on the unseen reality that was raging simultaneously. This can hardly be described as anything but intercession, or at the very least a prototype of intercession. We see clearly how that when one intervenes in the heavenly realms, God works in the course of earthly events.

Josh. 6: The first obstacle to entering Canaan, Jericho's walls were impregnable. The sword-wielding angel who encountered Joshua in 5:13-15 identified himself as "commander of the army of the LORD." When saying, "I have now come" (v. 14), he communicated that he had come for a military purpose and was ready for action. The ensuing confrontation was not humanly perceptible, but the seemingly ludicrous battle plans only emphasized the power of God when the walls collapsed.

2 Chron. 20: When a superior coalition army came against Jehoshaphat, he proclaimed a fast to inquire of the Lord. A prophecy was given, and all responded with worship. Their faith in the Lord was demonstrated by men going in front of the army to sing praise. The supernatural dimension was evident when the Lord set ambushes against the enemy and caused them to destroy each other. This is the clearest example of praise in holy warfare.

NEW TESTAMENT PRECEDENTS

Matt. 4:1-11 and Luke 4:1-13: Satan confronted Jesus himself, and his deception-based, would-be power over Jesus was effectively broken. This ordeal lasted a full 40 days (Luke 4:2). Jesus was first led by the Holy Spirit; then He prayed, fasted, and resisted Satan with the Word of God. Once Jesus overcame Satan, He launched His ministry of healing, teaching, and ultimately defeating Satan on the Cross.

Luke 10:17-20: The 72 returned describing the power of Jesus' name over evil spirits, and Jesus responded that He saw Satan fall like lightning from heaven, that He gave them authority over evil, and that nothing would harm them. This is a rather confrontational type of evangelism or holy warfare. He followed this affirmation by admonishing them against a fleshly response to this authority—their joy should be in the simple fact that their "names are written in heaven," not that they had spiritual power.

Acts 4:23-31: In the face of persecution, the Early Church modeled passionate intercession. They gave glory to God above all else and were faithful to put human acts within the context of God's greater purpose. Quoting Scripture was a significant part of their prayer. In presenting their problem to God, they asked for boldness in evangelism and power for signs and wonders.

Acts 13:4-12: As attendant to Sergius Paulus, the political leader of the island, Elymas very likely enjoyed some degree of influence over the area. Paul did not go against some unseen spiritual stronghold; he spoke to Elymas, the human vessel. When Elymas was blinded at Paul's rebuke, his power was obviously broken, and as a result Sergius Paulus believed in Jesus. This may have had ramifications upon those under his jurisdiction.

Acts 19: Ephesus was well known for its heavy spiritism and magical practices. In addition to Artemis, "at least forty-four other deities were worshiped in this city."[2] The scale of demonic activity was as intense here as anywhere else in Scripture. In the two years Paul stayed in Ephesus, his ministry was characterized by evangelism, healing, and deliverance. The outpouring of confession and burning of sorcery materials riled the shrine-maker Demetrius, who stirred up a crowd and caused great trouble.

APPLICATIONS

Applying Old Testament passages in a response to the cosmic powers, we find models of worship, prayer, shouting, and praising—but no direct confrontation with spirits themselves. That is left to God.

Applying New Testament passages in a response to the powers of darkness, we find models of extended prayer, fasting, and ordeals with the enemy; authority in Jesus' name and the importance of humble faith; use of Scripture; prayer for boldness and miracles; rebuking the human vessel of cosmic powers; personal evangelism; healing; and exorcism.

In all these models we find tremendous faith in God, total obedience, and lives set apart in holiness unto the Lord.

A significant parallel arises in three of the preceding passages. *Abram* saw the Canaanite-inhabited Promised Land for the first time and built an altar, giving praise to God. God's plan prevailed. *Joshua* physically led the people into the Promised Land, and the first thing he encountered was Jericho. Trusting only in the power of God, they overcame and entered the land. *Jesus* was about to enter into His earthly ministry, what might be called a spiritual Promised Land. He faced Satan himself and resisted his temptations. He went on to fulfill His work of salvation.

In each of the preceding instances, a power blocked the way. Each time the man of God took a stand. Each time God's people entered the new domain.

We should take three important points to heart. First, in every case it was God who initiated the action: He told Abram this would be his people's land. The angel of the Lord's army told Joshua he was there and ready to do warfare. The Holy Spirit led Jesus into the desert to fast, to pray, and to encounter the devil. Second, none of them ever went looking for spirits. Counting on them to obey His leading, God brought them to a new area where He wanted to build His kingdom. Third, opposition followed: famine struck Abram, and he faced possible death at Pharaoh's hand. Joshua's troops were routed at Ai because of Achan's sin. The people of Jesus' hometown, Nazareth, drove Him out and tried to kill Him.

BASIC PRINCIPLES

We do not find biblical figures spending much energy trying to discern the exact nature, names, or functions of spirits. While some will say that knowledge about a spirit gives one an advantage over it, the biblical model is to focus only on the power of God, which overcomes evil powers no matter what they are.

Throughout Scripture we see the importance of prayer and praise to God for winning the spiritual battle. We also see prophets, kings, Jesus, and the apostles directly confront evil by ministering to or confronting the human elements influenced by evil, whether false prophets, enemy armies, or afflicted individuals. But direct confrontation with the cosmic powers themselves is less common. For example, in the confrontation between the angel and the prince of Persia in Dan. 10:12-13, Daniel simply prayed and sought the Lord without any idea of what was happening.

On the personal level, we see Jesus all throughout the Gospels, and the apostles after him, binding demons and casting them out of people. Jesus and the apostles are direct and confrontational with demons or "unclean spirits" that afflict individuals. But with dark spiritual powers that affect people, organizations, localities, and societies on a broader scale, we do not see such direct assaults. In these cases, confrontation with forces of evil is more indirect, involving praise to God and appeals to God that God himself would bring them down.

At what point do we emphasize love, and at what point do we emphasize prayer to bind the powers of darkness? Scripture is consistent in showing us we are to love the individual or group who is deceived or lost in sin. We also see that there is a time for confrontation of sin and for rebuke—but even this must be done in love. When it comes to spiritual influences behind a person or group of people, love is never given to demons. Old Testament leaders appeal to the authority of God to destroy them, along with the people who oppose Israel. Jesus speaks directly and the apostles appeal to authority in Jesus' name to bind the powers of evil and stop them from their attempts to deceive and afflict. Simply, then, we are to love people and resist demons.

The weight of Scripture is on victory through obedient action, praise, and prayer to God, which go hand in hand with ministering the gospel and living a life of holiness and love. Direct confrontation with the powers of darkness is not prohibited, though as with the archangel Michael (Jude 9), we should be careful in this area. The most definitively confrontational exhortations are to "stand" firmly against the devil's schemes (Eph. 6:11, 13-14) and to "resist" the devil (James 4:7; 1 Pet. 5:9).

THE ARMOR OF GOD

The armor of God as described in Eph. 6:11-17 is central to holy warfare, but the metaphor of this spiritual armor is not simply something to "put on." It is an expression of our Christian identity and spiritual disposition. The parts of the armor need not be considered absolute metaphors, since 1 Thess. 5:8 speaks of "faith and love as a breastplate."

The six elements of the armor are commonly written about. Like a belt around us, we are to surround ourselves in God's truth for prevailing over Satan's deception. Righteousness, being justified through Jesus' blood and living in a right relation with God, covers us like a breastplate. Like having good shoes, we are to be always ready to act in ministering the gospel of peace; peacemaking and reconciliation are effective means of breaking the enemy's influence. To extinguish Satan's attacks (his flaming arrows), faith is a necessary shield; without faith we cannot please God or hope for victory. Assurance of salvation by grace is like the vital protection of a helmet, and with this we must always remember who we are in Christ. As a sword pierces, the Holy Spirit enlivens the Word of God for dramatic results; thus, we must know and apply Scripture.

These six areas of the Christian life are the way we are to carry out our "warfare." Yet with a slightly broader definition, two more elements become vital. In Eph. 6:18 and in the same paragraph, Paul exhorts us to pray in the Spirit. To do this, we must be yielded to God and follow the Holy Spirit's leading in prayer. The other element does not appear in this context but is given central importance throughout the New Testament and is part of the spiritual armor of 1 Thess. 5:8. In the same way he tells us to "put on" the armor, Paul writes in Col. 3:12-14 to "clothe yourselves" with attributes of the Christian life. He culminates this by saying, "over all these virtues put on love, which binds them all together in perfect unity." What we "wear" is incomplete without love, for without love we are nothing (1 Cor. 13:2).

Since Satan's battle is for the heart and mind, it is through action based on the dispositions of our heart and mind, as outlined in the armor, that we gain the victory. Our methods must not simply include this but be based on it and proceed from it.

POINTS TO REMEMBER IN HOLY WARFARE

Isa. 59:16 and 63:5 show us on one hand that God can deal with any problem without our getting involved. On the other hand, it indicates that He is "appalled" when we do not get involved. Ezek. 22:30 depicts God looking for a human vessel to intercede between Him and a problem. Throughout the biblical record we see that God's way is to work through people. His will is for us to participate with Him in His work on earth. To do this, we must grow in grace and maturity of faith.

Not all our problems are because of the devil. Don't give him more credit than he's worth! Scripture makes clear that human carnality is the root of most problems. Pride, selfishness, laziness, fear, anger, immorality, and greed cause plenty of problems with or without the help of any powers of darkness. Yet keep in mind the teaching of Eph. 2:1-3, that the world, the flesh, and the devil are so intertwined that you can hardly talk about one without talking about the others.

Your style of prayer is not as important as the condition of your heart. Knowing and living by your identity in Christ and maintaining holy intimacy with God are foundational to any victory, just as they are foundational to the Christian life. James 5:16 clearly says that "the prayer of a righteous man is powerful and effective." It says nothing about what actions or patterns the righteous man goes through. But so that we may have something to work with, I offer here some items that will be helpful to you in your holy warfare. Each one is the subject of entire books and is worthy of much attention. I condense them here in order to bring them together in a cohesive, usable approach.

Whatever scriptural promises or narratives we actually experience in our own lives, we experience on the same basis as our experience of salvation and everything else in the Christian life: we must appropriate them. That is, we receive the words of the Bible by faith and accept them as being for us here and now. What is ours in principle, as written in Scripture, we accept as ours personally and with practical application. Only when we take Bible promises and by faith make them our own do we truly experience them in our own lives.

LOVE ON ITS KNEES: PRAYER

When we pray intensely for someone or something, especially in a crisis, we are fighting for that person or purpose. We fight for people because we love them. My church and I fought not only for ourselves but also for our city, because we love our city and want people to know Jesus. The land adjacent to our church facility was only one day away from being sold to the largest Buddhist temple in the Western Hemisphere. We intervened with the landowner and began to fast and pray and walk the land, asking God to redeem it for His glory. We fought and agonized in prayer. My wife and I were ready to die for this, because we knew the potential impact a temple of that magnitude would have on our city and surrounding area. We recruited dozens of churches and scores of intercessors locally, regionally, and even internationally. Eventually God gave His peace to us concerning the battle. We then simply trusted Him, and soon the owner sold it instead to a real estate broker who subdivided it for the building of homes. If we had not fought the battle, we might be sitting next to a huge Buddhist temple that was expected to dominate the area. If God had not worked in the landowner's heart and mind, who knows what would have happened? As is the pattern throughout Scripture, we fight, and God brings the victory to those who believe. Our whole city has been impacted.

Prayer must be done in faith. Jesus often used the phrase "according to your faith." Rational analysis might find it hard to believe that malignant cancer will be healed or that a hardened community would yield a new work of the Holy Spirit. Simple, childlike faith is so important, for this is what moves mountains (Mark 11:22-26), and mountains are not things that are commonly moved. It is easy to analyze and criticize. But I, along with my church, have been learning simple, childlike faith, and the number of truly, medically verifiable healings has catapulted.

Prayer must be done with patience—lots of it. Luke 18:1-8 tells the parable of the persistent widow, after which Jesus essentially asks, "Do you pray like that?" God is looking for people who are persistent in prayer. If there were a club for those who were tired of waiting on God, it might have a chapter in every church. But in the persistence we are changed, and isn't that God's will?

Prayer is best spoken. Countless times I have caught myself dozing or mentally wandering when I prayed silently. Silent prayer has its place, but usually not in intercession. Praying out loud forces us to clarify our thoughts and say exactly what we mean, whereas silent prayer is free to float nebulously around in the mind. Spoken prayer also stimulates and energizes the person doing the praying. This is because speaking out loud helps focus one's attention, disallowing the mind to wander. The sound of one's own voice actually stimulates his or her ongoing prayer, particularly if it is done in earnest; silent prayer often tends to sedate the person.

Pray for yourself, your family, your community, your state or province, your nation, missionaries, and persecuted Christians. Pray for government leaders, legislation, and specific problems in your community or nation. Pray for your church, its members, outreach, internal problems, and its potentials. Some people use notebooks or prayer lists to help them remember everything; others pray more spontaneously. Pray also for a hunger for God, protection, and that God will bind the powers of darkness so that people may be free to turn to Him. Pray for pastors and spiritual leaders, that God would protect and empower them. You will find that the Bible either commands or gives examples of praying for all of these.

Being Specific

Generalities might blast a wide area, but they have little effect. How will *O God, bless the world!* ever be answered? Specific prayers are like a high-powered rifle—the target is much more carefully and knowledgeably discerned, and the resulting impact is far greater. *O God, bring reconciliation between John and Suzie!* is a prayer that will go somewhere. Specific prayers focus attention and faith on the subject, and they are much more likely to endure to an answer than generalized prayers, in which you can't really assess whether the prayer is being answered.

Generalities soon cause the intercessor to lose interest, because it is difficult to know whether a prayer is answered. In fact, if a prayer is vague, it can't really be answered or unanswered, and the intercessor easily loses motivation and direction. So be as specific as possible about the problem and the desired outcome. Even if the Lord leads differently, because you're being specific, you will better discern how the Lord is working.

The Blood of Christ

The blood of Christ is frequently referred to in the New Testament. The importance of the blood is clarified back in Lev. 17:11, which speaks of animal sacrifice: "It is the blood that makes atonement for one's life." Heb. 9:14 speaks of how the blood of Christ cleanses us "through the eternal Spirit." His blood sacrifice is therefore for all time. Thus, it is through the blood of Christ, signifying His death in our place, that we are redeemed (Eph. 1:7). We are justified by His blood (Rom. 5:9). The blood of Jesus "purifies us from all sin" (1 John 1:7), and we are made holy "through his own blood" (Heb. 13:12). These verses testify to the grace we receive from God, which saves us and makes us His own.

In holy warfare it is critical to stand on the basics of what God has done for us. The devil would be pleased if we really didn't believe that we were saved and sanctified. If he deceives us into thinking so, he robs us of our confidence in what God has done for us and in who we are in Christ. That, of course, would make us totally ineffective, and he surely knows that. Lev. 17:11 states that "the life of a creature is in the blood." Thus, when blood is shed, the life is given up for the benefactor. The blood of Christ is the crux of the fact that Christ gave His life for us, so that we could live our lives in Him. This is the foundation of our whole Christian life.

Relating to holy warfare, Rev. 12:11 proclaims, "They overcame [the devil] by the blood of the Lamb and by the word of their testimony." It is Christ's sacrificial death on the Cross, the shedding of His blood in the giving of His life, and His resurrection to absolute sovereignty that overthrows Satan.

The Word of God

In the armor of God, Scripture is referred to as an offensive weapon (Eph. 6:17). We are to ask God to work according to His Word; indeed, He seems to wait for us to do so, wanting us to be involved in His work on earth.

Jesus used Scripture when resisting the devil. At all three points of His wilderness temptation Jesus responded, "It is written. . . . It is . . . written. . . . It is written" (Matt. 4:4, 7, 10). Satan could not stand against the Word of God or someone who stood firmly on it.

To pray the Scriptures is to quote them back to God in prayer. This is not for God's benefit, but for our benefit, because it affirms our faith in His promises. Praying according to Scripture is appealing to God to do what He has promised to do in His Word. Praying the Scripture lends itself to praying according to God's will. This is because we are praying what

God's Word actually says He wills or will do. We only need to be careful with the application.

The prayer of the believers in Acts 4:23-31 is an example of praying according to Scripture. Peter and John returned to the believers after having been threatened by the Sanhedrin. They quoted David's words in Ps. 2:1-2, applied it to their present situation with Pilate, the Gentiles, and the people of Israel, then asked God in response to bestow boldness and miraculous power through the name of Jesus. God answered.

The Name of Jesus

A name is the verbal representation of a person. In Scripture it is also a representation of that person's character and identity. "Jesus" (Y'shua) means "Yahweh is Salvation." Phil. 2:10 says that "at the name of Jesus every knee should bow, in heaven and on earth and under the earth." When we pray or speak in Jesus' name, we speak by His authority, which is absolute. If we have a problem, it is because we are not absolute.

When we speak in Jesus' name, we speak by His authority. In Mark 16:17 Jesus lists things we will do in His name. In Acts 3:6 Peter healed the lame man "in the name of Jesus Christ of Nazareth." In Acts 4:7 the Sanhedrin interrogated Peter and John by asking, "By what power or what name did you do this?" Peter's Spirit-filled response is that it was "by the name of Jesus Christ of Nazareth" that he had healed the lame man (v. 10) and that "there is no other name" by which to be saved (v. 12).

Praying in Jesus' name should not be a mechanical attachment to our prayers. Rather, it is praying in confidence under the authority of the One we follow. When we pray in Jesus' name, we pray with Jesus' authority.

Fasting and Prayer

Fasting in its broadest definition is the voluntary denial of something one normally does (usually eating), for the sake of intensifying a spiritual endeavor (usually prayer). Fasting itself does little but shed weight, but fasting with a purpose injects intensity into that purpose and is often part of positive results. Not too many of us rejoice at the opportunity to fast, but it is an important part of an effective prayer life.

Biblical examples provide at least three general reasons for fasts. One was for mourning and grief over death or a great loss (see Neh. 1:1-4). Another was for humbling oneself and repenting (see Dan. 9:1-3). The most broad and the most common was for petition (see 2 Chron. 20:1-4). Petition can be for guidance, protection, forgiveness, understanding, spiritual empowerment, or healing.

Throughout Scripture, fasting is an act of humility before God. It is a time for examining one's life. And it certainly is a time of intensified seeking of God. Isa. 58 describes the way in which acts of mercy and social justice are to be part of fasting, an injunction too often forgotten.

Absolute fasts are when one does not eat or drink anything at all for the time determined. Partial fasts can be done many ways: some will refrain from foods but drink liquids; others may refrain from certain types of food. How long a person fasts is up to his or her discretion, but beginners might start fasting one meal and work up to a day, then several days. Fasting may be done while going through normal daily functions, although, whenever possible, it is good to get away from the daily busyness of life to focus on prayer.

Regardless of how it is done, fasting has the effect of intensifying one's prayer. An empty stomach focuses one's prayer, because it is a constant reminder of what he or she is praying for. The hunger may be intense or dull, but for most people it doesn't go completely away. It is a physical way of expressing to the Lord, "I'm really serious about this!"

Daniel engaged in a partial fast for three weeks (Dan. 10:2-3). Unbeknownst to him, his activity was related to activity in the spiritual realm. A demonic spirit actually hindered his prayer, and the spiritual battle is later described to him (vv. 12-13). Most people who are serious about holy warfare innately know the value of fasting. Fasting is one of those things that in order to be understood must be done, not just talked about—like prayer itself. Those who fast seriously and with spiritual motives generally find that it opens up dimensions to their Christian lives largely unobtainable in any other way. Those dimensions may be in the area of power, spiritual break-throughs, wisdom, commitment, faith, victory, consecration and holiness, or self-discipline.

Group Intercession

In Acts 4:24 the believers "raised their voices together in prayer." Prayer is something the Church must do not just in the privacy of people's own homes, but together as a group. Jesus says, "Where two or three come together in my name, there am I with them" (Matt. 18:20). Hearing others pray, being prayed for, and joining others in praying over a subject stimulate not only the individual's prayer but also the commitment to pray as part of a corporate body of believers holding a common bond and purpose.

My experience is probably similar to that in most churches: the biggest difficulty in praying as a church is not getting it organized but getting people motivated. If people are motivated, it doesn't much matter if they pray in pairs or around a circle, whether they pray in home cell groups or in Sunday School. Perhaps the best motivator to prayer is *answered* prayer. Tell about every answer to prayer—celebrate them! As people see and experience answered prayer, whatever it concerns, it increases their faith and expectation. When they pray with fervency or conviction, they pray effectively.

Make prayer a part of every church gathering. Leaders in the church, starting with the pastor, need to set the example.

Prayer should be an important part of Sunday worship (not just listening to the pastor pray). Prayer at the altar can include intercession; prayer requests can be given and prayed for; people can turn and pray with those seated next to them. Early-morning prayer, late-night prayer, prayer chains, prayer in home cell groups, and prayer walks are ways our church prays together. Every church will find ways that fit it the best.

Prayer Walks

In Josh. 1:3 God promised to give Joshua every place where he set his foot. A prayer walk is taking prayer out of the four walls of the church by simply taking a walk with the purpose of praying. For example, while walking in a certain place, one prays for those who live there. Prayer walking breaks down the walls of the church by taking the congregation out of their enclosed meetings into the outside world. This increases our concern for and awareness of the community, because we are deliberately walking through it, seeking God on its behalf.

We do prayer walks around and through our church facility every Sunday morning, asking for God's blessing. We no longer feel the sense of spiritual darkness or heaviness that we once did. We did extensive prayer walking in the battle over the land next door to us. We fasted and walked daily until we sensed a release from the Lord and the peace that He would take care of it. On an ongoing basis some walk through surrounding neighborhoods and ask God to open the people's spiritual eyes or to give them a hunger or a desire to know God. We pray for blessing, the withholding of evil, hunger for God, for the Lord to work on non-Christians, and for the undoing of sinful establishments.

Teams of two are usually recommended for prayer walks. First, because two are obviously safer than one (in tough neighborhoods you may want even larger groups). Second, if you go by yourself, outside observers may think you are talking to yourself and are mentally unbalanced!

Prayer walks can be simple walks through surrounding neighborhoods, or they can become involved, long-distance hikes across many miles. They can be done individually during the normal routines of life, or they can be planned group activities. Some take "prayer journeys," in which they go as tourists to an unevangelized part of the world and pray there. The wonderful thing about prayer is that it knows no boundaries.

The Power of Praise

Ps. 8:2 proclaims, "From the lips of children and infants you have ordained praise because of your enemies, to silence the foe and the avenger." The power of praise rests not on maturity or understanding but on the heart. It rests on faith not on reason, for often it seems unreasonable. Jehoshaphat experienced the power of praise overcoming the enemy when God literally routed Ammon, Moab, and Mount Seir in response to Israel's praise. Biblically, then, the very act of praising God is a kind, or important part, of holy warfare.

Whether the words are in a hymnal or are projected onto a screen is irrelevant. What is relevant is whether the praise is from the heart and lifts us up into God's presence. You can simply sing, or you can truly worship. True praise and worship moves us beyond our daily, earthly existence, beyond logical discussion to a deep intimacy with God. Such intimacy is crucial to a believer's strength and victory.

As we praise God, there is a sense in which He becomes to us what we praise Him for. As we praise Him for being our strong fortress, we are reminded of His strength. When we praise Him for being our joy, our victory, our peace, our healer, our sanctifier, we are drawn into spiritual communion with Him and with open hearts receive the blessing we praise Him for. As we experience what we praise Him for, we are more able to gain victory over the enemy's opposition.

Knowing What We're Praying About

Lord, deal with the sin in our community is vague. What kind of sin is it? Violence? Prostitution and pornography? Alcoholism? Racism? Homosexuality? Materialism? People do not sin vaguely. Sin is a specific, identifiable thought or action. The Old Testament prophets did not vaguely denounce the sins of Israel or of any other nation. They specifically identified the sins God was angry about.

Learn your community's history and how it got that way. One of our church members lives on top of what was once a cemetery. Strange phenomena occurred with them and their neighbors. Rather than debate the issue, we took authority in Jesus' name and asked God to bring everything under submission to Christ. God answered our prayer. In the same way learn your church's history. Do any patterns of sin or problems stick out? We had them. They defined much of what we prayed about, and we learned to pray as specifically as possible that these patterns would be overcome. Specific prayer goes deeper than vague prayer, is more powerful, more inspiring to the person who prays, and engenders more continuity over the long haul. And face it—the problems and sins we confront in our society are often formidable and require enduring prayer.

Discerning to the best of your ability any outstanding tendencies or types of sin helps you see the modus operandi of evil forces in the human realm. This enables you to see the way Paul saw when he recognized that "our struggle is not against flesh and blood." If your church or community has a particularly tainted history, or if certain sins or problems are outstanding or chronic, these will help define what you pray about. Changes in people or the community then become indicators as to how much your prayer is being answered.

Listening to God's Leading

I prayed with a well-known intercessor who spent half of his prayer time listening. He just sat there and waited upon God. He said there was no use in praying something that wasn't God's will. He said if you discerned God's will first, your prayer would be far more effective and would more likely be answered. Spend time just waiting upon the Lord, as the psalmists often did. Only then can you slow down and unclutter your mind enough to discern how the Lord may lead you. He may prompt you in some way or lead you to think or feel a certain way. Take those things seriously and test them. If indications are that the Lord is leading this way, pursue it. Power in prayer comes not from sweating or speaking in an authoritative-sounding voice. Power in prayer comes from praying according to God's will, which is a basic condition for receiving God's answer (1 John 5:14-15). Take time to discern what His will may be, and don't be fearful of correction.

Prayer should be "in the Spirit" according to Eph. 6:18 and Jude 20. That is, rather than praying according to our personal desires or our preconceived lists, our prayer is to be filled with the presence and leading of the Holy Spirit. People use many terms for prayer according to the leading of the Spirit: "burdened," "prompted," "led," and so on. You may or may not have any particular feelings or spiritual impressions when you pray. If you don't, that's all right. If you do, the Bible says to test them. Perhaps the Lord is leading you, or perhaps it's something you ate for lunch. Discerning God's leading often takes time and trials, and sometimes it may not be there. But ask God for the presence and leading of His Holy Spirit when you pray.

LOVE IN ACTION: LIFESTYLE

I will not attempt to outline here the Holiness lifestyle. This has sufficiently been done in countless other writings. The point here is that our lifestyle is an integral part of holy warfare, not something in addition to it. The way we live is not extra or separate from holy warfare; it *is* holy warfare, just as prayer is holy warfare. It may be easy for some to think that all we need to do is pray, and how we live our lives is something else. I have prayed for years with coalitions of believers seeking revival and the overthrow of demonic powers. Observation has often led me to suspect that deep down many have hoped that through their prayer alone God would change everything and people would be swept into the church—thus, they would not have to go through the nitty-gritty of genuinely living out the Christian life. I have never seen God let that happen. God is not in the business of giving shortcuts, for they are disastrous in the Christian life.

Churches that most often see great works of God are those whose prayer arises out of a lifestyle of sacrificial love and obedience. These churches are most frequently suffering churches, where they are persecuted for their faith or where socioeconomic conditions cause everyone to suffer. They are not seduced by the complacency that besets churches in free, highly developed nations. Yet even in the free, highly developed nations of Europe, North America, and parts of Asia, believers can, and do, make the choice of sacrificial love and obedience in their daily lives. And they do so knowing, and in every new case expecting, that the powers of darkness cannot stand against the unfailing love of God expressed through believers. You may be one of these people. If not, you can be.

On a mission trip to India, my partner and I chose to love the people by living with them, sleeping on their dirt floors, eating their food with them, wearing the same clothes they wore, and possessing little more than they had themselves. We got sick a lot. But we found that Jesus' words to Paul are true: "My power is made perfect in weakness" (2 Cor. 12:9). My weakness opened to me an intimacy with God I had never had before. From that my whole daily life intensified with the presence of God and His purpose. Back in the United States, my wife said that if her husband was going to live like that, far be it from her to sleep on our comfortable bed. Her act of love was to sleep on the floor for two months and intercede in fervent prayer for me. I returned with tears of joy at over a hundred conversions, many healings, and pastors and churches touched and changed by the power of God. People's hearts open when they encounter persistent, genuine, sacrificial Christian love. I believe God is pleased to respond to such love too.

Simply being good does not necessarily mean one experiences overcoming power. The power of holiness is found in heart purity *with a purpose.* Goodness has to be good for something; otherwise, it is purely theoretical. A self-absorbed holiness is really not holiness at all; it is self-centered personal piety. The Pharisees who opposed Jesus had that, and Jesus rebuked them. Heart purity with a purpose fills the life of the individual and projects that life to others, because love compels one to care about others and to share the love of God with them.

On issues that affect moral directions, we must take a stand in our family, church, community, state or province, and nation. Love does not hide from or ignore evil; it takes a stand. In personal relations, love compels us to pursue peace, forgiveness, and reconciliation. The biblical concept of peace, *shalom,* means that there is well-being in all areas of one's life. With personal morals and convictions, love for God puts His ways above carnal desires, and love for others and ourselves puts their and our well-being before the object of desire. You'll need lots of patience when it looks as if your efforts are going nowhere. But a lifestyle of Christian love is purposeful unto itself, even if great gains are not made in holy warfare. Holy warfare, on the other hand, will not have much effect without a lifestyle of love.

Remember that holy people are dangerous to the devil. Evil spirits can't get a foothold in the lives of people who have pure hearts before God, who confess what needs to be confessed, and who seek intimacy with God. These are people the devil has a hard time tempting, people who know God's will, follow it, and share it with others. These people are dangerous to the devil, because he can't get the better of them—they get the better of *him.*

The devil can overrun personal piety, but he has a hard time against genuine love. How do we love? We love by giving and forgiving. We love by spending time and money, by tears, by loving embraces, by bearing burdens, and by indignation at evil. My wife and I—especially my wife—have won many spiritual battles through love. Love can be expensive. It can keep us up late with someone. It can be a bother and a hassle. But it has no substitute or alternative. And that is God's intention. Jesus makes clear in John 13:34-35 that loving others is the trademark of a disciple. He knew and demonstrated how costly love can be.

With enough love we could conquer the world. But love does not conquer—it suffers. That is how it remains love. John Dawson writes, "Love is measured and demonstrated by sacrifice—by costly action. Love continues no matter what the cost. 'Greater love has no one than this, than to lay down one's life for his friends' (John 15:13). Love identifies with suffering and endures until it is ended."[3]

Victory comes to those who endure and prevail. It is through the battles of life that the Lord builds our character and Christian maturity. Battles leave us with scars, and that puts us in good company with Him who won the ultimate battle when love was nailed to the Cross.

Notes

Chapter 1

1. John Wesley, *The Works of John Wesley* (Grand Rapids: William B. Eerdmans Publishing Co., 1958), 6:371.

2. Richard S. Taylor, *The Theological Formulation,* vol. 3 of *Exploring Christian Holiness* (Kansas City: Beacon Hill Press of Kansas City, 1985), 213.

3. Donald Hohensee, "The Holy Spirit and Power: A Wesleyan Understanding," in *Wrestling with Dark Angels: Toward a Deeper Understanding of the Supernatural Forces in Spiritual Warfare,* comps. C. Peter Wagner and F. Douglas Pennoyer (Ventura, Calif.: Regal Books, 1990), 174.

4. C. S. Lewis, *The Screwtape Letters,* rev. ed. (New York: Macmillan, 1982), 3.

5. Melvin Dieter, "The Wesleyan Perspective," in *Five Views of Sanctification,* ed. Melvin Dieter (Grand Rapids: Zondervan Publishing House, 1987), 11.

Chapter 2

1. Peter O'Brien, "Principalities and Powers: Opponents of the Church," in *Biblical Interpretation and the Church: The Problem of Contextualization,* ed. D. A. Carson (Nashville: Thomas Nelson Publishers, 1984), 111.

2. Gregory A. Boyd, *God at War: The Bible and Spiritual Conflict* (Downers Grove, Ill.: InterVarsity Press, 1997), 293.

3. Mildred Bangs Wynkoop, *Foundations of Wesleyan-Arminian Theology* (Kansas City: Beacon Hill Press of Kansas City, 1967), 98.

4. Robert Hillman, "Grace in the Preaching of Calvin and Wesley: A Comparative Study" (Ph.D. diss., Fuller Theological Seminary, 1978), 351.

5. E. Stanley Jones, *A Song of Ascents* (Nashville: Abingdon Press, 1968), 57.

6. Wesley, *Works,* 5:296-97.

7. Hillman, "Calvin and Wesley," 351.

8. Wesley, *Works,* 6:413.

9. W. T. Purkiser, Richard S. Taylor, and Willard H. Taylor, *God,*

Man, and Salvation: A Biblical Theology (Kansas City: Beacon Hill Press of Kansas City, 1977), 469-70.

10. Dick Eastman, *Love on Its Knees* (Old Tappan, N.J.: Chosen Books, 1989), 28.

Chapter 3

1. Paul Hiebert, *Anthropological Insights for Missionaries* (Grand Rapids: Baker Book House, 1985), 45.

2. "Worldview and Worldview Change MB725" (syllabus, Fuller Theological Seminary, 1989), 38.

3. Paul Hiebert, "The Flaw of the Excluded Middle," *Missiology* 10 (1982): 1, 43.

4. Boyd, *God at War,* 140.

5. Paul Hiebert, "Epistemological Foundations for Science and Theology," *Theological Student's Fellowship Bulletin* 8 (March-April 1985): 5-10.

6. In relation to the text itself, certain fallacies should be guarded against. Grant Osborne outlines them well, and I note six major ones here.

Lexical fallacy: to assume that word studies can settle theological arguments. *Root fallacy:* [assuming] the root of a term . . . is reflected in every subordinate use of the word(s). *Misuse of subsequent meaning:* when we read later meanings back into the biblical material. *One-meaning fallacy:* the view that every appearance of a Hebrew or Greek term should be translated by the same English word. *Misuse of parallels:* [supporting one's interpretation with scriptural] parallels which would support [one's] preconceived notions. *Ignoring the context:* [a common error that makes the others possible in the first place] a word-by-word approach . . . usually isolates each word from the other terms surrounding it and as a result fails to put the message of the text together as a coherent whole. (*The Hermeneutical Spiral* [Downers Grove, Ill.: InterVarsity Press, 1991], 65-75.)

Chapter 4

1. *I and II Kings*, Old Testament Library (Philadelphia: Westminster Press, 1964), 490.

2. G. H. Jones describes each god and the characteristics associated with it. All are quite distinctive. See *1 and 2 Kings*, vol. 2 of *New Century Bible Commentary* (Grand Rapids: William B. Eerdmans Publishing Co., 1984), 554-55.

3. *2 Chronicles*, *Word Biblical Commentary* (Waco, Tex.: Word Books, 1987), 201.

4. *Interpreter's Dictionary of the Bible* (Nashville: Abingdon Press, 1962), 1:376.

5. *Biblical Commentary on the Book of Daniel* (Grand Rapids: William B. Eerdmans Publishing Co., 1949), 416.

Chapter 5

1. Gerhard Kittel, ed., *A Theological Dictionary of the New Testament* (Grand Rapids: William B. Eerdmans Publishing Co., 1964), 1:479.

2. Ibid., 3:891.

3. I am using the letter *w* to signify the Greek letter omega, which has a long *o* sound, distinct from the short *o* of the omicron.

4. Kittel, *Theological Dictionary,* 2:2.

5. Ibid., 6-8.

6. Ibid., 573.

7. Ibid., 562.

8. Clinton E. Arnold, *Ephesians: Power and Magic: The Concept of Power in Ephesians in Light of Its Historical Setting* (Grand Rapids: Baker Books, 1992), 53.

9. Kittel, *Theological Dictionary,* 3:634.

10. Jung Young Lee, "Interpreting the Demonic Powers in Pauline Thought," *Novum Testamentum* 12 (1970): 60.

11. Kittel, *Theological Dictionary,* 5:590.

12. Arnold, *Power and Magic,* 68.

13. Lee, "Interpreting the Demonic," 61.

14. Colin Brown, *The New International Dictionary of New Testament Theology* (Grand Rapids: William B. Eerdmans Publishing Co., 1976), 2:451.

15. Kittel, *Theological Dictionary,* 3:166-67.

16. Walter Bauer, *A Greek-English Lexicon of the New Testament and Other Early Christian Literature,* 2nd ed. (Chicago: University of Chicago Press, 1979), 805.

17. Ibid., 62-63.

18. Andrew Lincoln, *Ephesians, Word Biblical Commentary* (Waco, Tex.: Word Books, 1990), 188-89.

19. Ibid., 443.

20. Oscar Cullmann, *The State in the New Testament* (London: SCM Press, 1956), 100.

21. G. H. C. MacGregor, "Principalities and Powers: The Cosmic Background of Paul's Thought," *New Testament Studies* 1 (1955): 24.

22. Ibid., 61.

23. Robert Mounce, *The Book of Revelation, New International Commentary on the New Testament* (Grand Rapids: William B. Eerdmans Publishing Co., 1977), 96.

24. Ibid., 96-97.

Chapter 6

1. See G. B. Caird (*Principalities and Powers* [Oxford, England: Clarendon Press, 1956], 20-28); Markus Barth (*The Broken Wall: A Study of the Epistle to the Ephesians* [Valley Forge, Pa.: Judson Press, 1959], 90); Heinrich Schlier (*Principalities and Powers in the New Testament* [New York: Harder and Harder, 1961], 31-32); and Hendrikus Berkhof (*Christ and the Powers* [Scottdale, Pa.: Herald Press, 1962], 25 ff.). Caird and Barth later modified their theories when writing commentaries on Ephesians and recognized the powers as spiritual. In a related position, Wesley Carr (*Angels and Principalities* [Cambridge, England: Cambridge University Press, 1981]) rejects the existence of demonic powers now or then, saying that evil was personified only in Satan and that the cosmic powers were all good angels.

2. Writing against the background of South American dictatorships, he sees dark powers as "the inner or spiritual essence, or gestalt, of an institution or state or system" (*The Powers,* vol. 1 of *Naming the Powers* [Philadelphia: Fortress Press, 1984], 104). He interprets "demons" as "the psychic or spiritual power emanated by organizations or individuals" (104) and "Satan" as the "power that congeals around collective idolatry, injustice, or inhumanity" (105). Wink openly claims that the dark powers do not "have a separate, spiritual existence" (105). He interprets heavenly angels the same way (104), never taking seriously their biblically stated supernatural aspects.

3. John Yoder, *The Politics of Jesus* (Grand Rapids: William B. Eerdmans Publishing Co., 1972), 150-52.

4. O'Brien, "Principalities and Powers," 61.

5. Oscar Cullmann, *Christ and Time* (London: SCM Press, 1951), 195.

6. Wesley, *Works,* 6:347.

7. Michael Green, *I Believe in Satan's Downfall* (Grand Rapids: William B. Eerdmans Publishing Co., 1981), 217.

8. Tom White, *Breaking Strongholds: How Spiritual Warfare Sets Captives Free* (Ann Arbor, Mich.: Vine Books, 1993), 24.

9. Brown, *New International Dictionary,* 2:200.

Chapter 7

1. Paul Hiebert, "Spiritual Warfare: Biblical Perspectives," *Mission Focus* 20:3 (1992), 43.

2. Clinton Arnold, *Powers of Darkness: Principalities and Powers in Paul's Letters* (Downers Grove, Ill.: InterVarsity Press, 1992), 150.

3. John Dawson, *Taking Our Cities for God* (Lake Mary, Fla.: Creation House, 1989), 212.

Select Bibliography

Arnold, Clinton E. *Ephesians: Power and Magic: The Concept of Power in Ephesians in Light of Its Historical Setting.* Grand Rapids: Baker Books, 1992.

————. *Powers of Darkness: Principalities and Powers in Paul's Letters.* Downers Grove, Ill.: InterVarsity Press, 1992.

Beckett, Bob. *Commitment to Conquer.* Grand Rapids: Chosen Books, 1997.

Boyd, Gregory A. *God at War: The Bible and Spiritual Conflict.* Downers Grove, Ill.: InterVarsity Press, 1997.

Bubeck, Mark I. *The Adversary.* Chicago: Moody Press, 1975.

————. *Overcoming the Adversary.* Chicago: Moody Press, 1984.

————. *Preparing for Battle: A Spiritual Warfare Workbook.* Chicago: Moody Press, 1999.

Dawson, John. *Taking Our Cities for God.* Lake Mary, Fla.: Creation House, 1989.

Eastman, Dick. *Love on Its Knees.* Old Tappan, N.J.: Chosen Books, 1989.

Green, Michael. *I Believe in Satan's Downfall.* Grand Rapids: William B. Eerdmans Publishing Co., 1981.

Haggard, Ted. *Primary Purpose.* Orlando, Fla.: Creation House, 1995.

Hiebert, Paul. *Anthropological Insights for Missionaries.* Grand Rapids: Baker Book House, 1985.

————. "The Flaw of the Excluded Middle," *Missiology* 10 (1982).

Jacobs, Cindy. *Possessing the Gates of the Enemy.* Tarrytown, N.Y.: Chosen Books, 1991.

Kendrick, Graham, and John Houghton. *Prayer Walking.* Eastbourne, United Kingdom: Kingsway Publications, 1990.

Kittel, Gerhard, ed. *A Theological Dictionary of the New Testament.* Grand Rapids: William B. Eerdmans Publishing Co., 1964-74.

Kraft, Charles. *Christianity with Power.* Ann Arbor, Mich.: Servant Publications, 1989.

McAlpine, Thomas. *Facing the Powers: What Are the Options?* Monrovia, Calif.: MARC, 1991.

Murphy, Ed. *The Handbook for Spiritual Warfare.* Nashville: Thomas Nelson Publishers, 1996.

O'Brien, Peter. "Principalities and Powers: Opponents of the Church," in *Biblical Interpretation and the Church: The Problem of Contextualization.* Ed. D. A. Carson. Nashville: Thomas Nelson Publishers, 1984.

Otis, George, Jr. *Informed Intercession: Transforming Your Community Through Spiritual Mapping and Strategic Power.* Ventura, Calif.: Gospel Light Publications, 1999.

Powlison, David. *Power Encounters: Reclaiming Spiritual Warfare.* Grand Rapids: Baker Book House, 1994.

Sheets, Dutch. *Intercessory Prayer.* Ventura, Calif.: Regal Books, 1996.

Teykl, Terry. *Pray and Grow.* Nashville: Discipleship Resources, 1988.

Wagner, C. Peter. *Breaking Strongholds in Your City.* Ventura, Calif.: Regal Books, 1993.

————. *Prayer Shield.* Ventura, Calif.: Regal Books, 1992.

————. *Warfare Prayer.* Ventura, Calif.: Regal Books, 1992.

Wagner, C. Peter, and F. Douglas Pennoyer, eds. *Wrestling with Dark Angels.* Ventura, Calif.: Regal Books, 1990.

Warner, Timothy M. *Spiritual Warfare.* Wheaton, Ill.: Crossway Books, 1991.

Wesley, John. *The Works of John Wesley.* Grand Rapids: William B. Eerdmans Publishing Co., 1958.

White, Tom. *The Believer's Guide to Spiritual Warfare.* Ann Arbor, Mich.: Vine Books, 1990.

————. *Breaking Strongholds: How Spiritual Warfare Sets Captives Free.* Ann Arbor, Mich.: Vine Books, 1993.